KEEPING YOUR CHURCH SAFE

Security Essentials for Houses of Worship

2ND EDITION

by Ron Aguiar

MY KIDS CALL ME "CAPTAIN SAFETY."
I'm the guy who sits facing the front door in a restaurant. I'm also the one who looks for at least two emergency exits in every large room — one primary and the other secondary, in case the first is blocked. My wife and I recently watched our three-and-a-half-year-old grandson while my daughter was out of town. As we drove him to his pre-school one morning, he dropped his sippy cup and asked us to pick it up. He was buckled in his car seat so he couldn't reach it. I was driving, so my wife tried to get it, but it was out of reach. She unbuckled her seat belt, reached back and retrieved the cup. While she was doing this, he said: "Nanny, put your seat belt on." I loved it.

I write a lot about teaching and training in this book. I hope you take that seriously. Pass on what you learn and keep returning to reinforce the lessons taught. I can't thank the men and women of the Honolulu Police Department enough for instilling life lessons during my time with the department. The training never stopped, from my first day as a cadet to my last day as an officer. There were many times I instinctively did what I was taught to protect myself and others around me. Keep your house of worship safe by doing the same with your team, staff and volunteers.

Ron Aguiar
Founder and CEO — Oasis Safety

Printed in the United States

ISBN 978-0-9967874-9-9

Keeping Your Church Safe
Second Edition

Written by Ron Aguiar

Cover Designed by Kelly Welke

Designed by Kelly Welke

www.USCCA.com

I want to thank my family — my wife, Nancy, and my children, Becky and Scott. I love you all. Nan, you are a great wife, mother and grandmother. Jesus lives in you, and it shows. Becky, I am so proud of you as you raise Silas in a Godly home. Continue to use your strength, courage and discernment as you follow God's leading. Scott, your compassion and leadership skills serve you well. Listen to the Lord for his guidance as your circle of influence grows. I am proud of you.

To the USCCA, thank you for allowing me to share my words, so houses of worship can keep themselves safe. You've made me feel part of the family. Keep up the excellent work in teaching, training and showing people how to protect themselves and their families.

To my Lord and Savior, Jesus Christ, gratitude and love for allowing me to be an instrument used on your behalf.

ACKNOWLEDGMENTS

CONTENTS

1 CHAPTER ONE

If any of you lacks wisdom, he should ask God, who gives generously to all without finding fault, and it will be given to him.

JAMES 1:5 (NIV)

A person or organization manages risk by **accepting, transferring, controlling or avoiding** an event. Let me explain. Do you know a cigarette smoker? As precious as life is to all of us — and understanding the risks associated with smoking — do you think a smoker's objective in life is to die an early death from lung cancer? I doubt it.

If a person refuses to quit or has given up trying to stop despite proof that smoking cigarettes causes cancer, then he or she has **accepted** the risk of smoking and the associated risk of early death as a consequence of the choice to continue the destructive habit. Consider my friend Tom, for example. When he decided to keep smoking and ignore his doctor's advice, he **transferred** some of that risk by taking out an insurance policy that will help pay for the high medical costs associated with the risk of smoking.

If, on the other hand, Tom decides to quit and is successful in doing so, he is taking measures to **control** the risk associated with smoking. His healthy choice to stop smoking lowers future chances of getting cancer. Although his decision to quit smoking may not prevent cancer, Tom's decision eliminates future actions that could contribute to complications associated with smoking.

If Tom had never smoked, then he would have **avoided** the risks associated with smoking.

SO … HOW DO YOU MANAGE RISK?

ACCEPT
TRANSFER
CONTROL
AVOID

IDENTIFYING THE RISK

First and foremost, determine the level of risk associated with the circumstance or the event causing the threat. After you have identified the danger, collect as much information as possible to assess the extent of the risk before deciding if action is warranted. You may receive information in a variety of ways. A safety committee or safety officer may point it out during a routine inspection. A visitor or congregation member may bring the item to your attention. Of course, the concern may not be a single safety issue like a broken door or slippery walkway. The risk may be an event such as a teen concert or a senior adult recreation trip. If you're asked to approve an event, you should first consider any risks involved before going forward.

TREATING THE RISK

Once the event or concern is acknowledged, evaluate any risks. Ask questions. Do we have enough security to handle the crowd? Do we need to have medical staff on site to treat any injury or illness? Before approving an event, address these two questions. Ask yourself what you are **reasonably expected** to provide to create a safe and secure environment.

Always ask: "Have I done everything reasonably expected to provide adequate services to reduce any risk associated with the event?" If the answer is no, do not hold the event.

EXAMPLE ONE MANAGING RISK

Someone in your church suggests that you create an adult basketball league to expand the sports ministry. During the process of approving the league, you look at some of the risks associated with the endeavor:

- When and where will the games be held?
- Do the rules consider the age of the group playing?
- Does funding cover costs associated with running the league? (Referee salaries, insurance costs, etc.)
- What preparations do you need to handle injuries?
- What preparations should you make to handle disputes?
- Who will officiate and manage the league?
- Should non-members or guests be allowed to play?
- Do you have sufficient insurance coverage?
- If physical injury occurs, will medical bills and punitive damages be covered?
- Is a leased, non-church-owned facility in good enough condition to handle the intended use?

In this example of the basketball league, consider a few suggestions to reduce your risk:

- As part of the registration process, have participants read and sign a release form that reduces the church's liability in cases of injury or death. Work with an attorney to draft the release form.
- Hold an informational meeting with all players before the first game to review rules and regulations.
- Hire trained and certified referees to officiate all games.
- Have a league coordinator or staff member on site to handle any disputes.

- Have a first-aid kit and AED available, along with a medically trained professional.

- When leasing an off-site facility, make sure its physical condition accommodates usage (e.g., adequate parking, no leaking roof, adequate bathroom facilities, proper lighting, etc.).

Following these suggestions can reduce your exposure to risk. Naturally, you hope nobody gets hurt during any of the games. But you have trained personnel to administer first aid, just in case. If a disagreement on the court leads to physical confrontation, a referee or staff person can intervene. The reasonable and prudent preventive measures you take help to protect everyone from bodily injury and the church from civil litigation.

EXAMPLE TWO MANAGING RISK

The safety officer points out children playing on the church's playground. He feels the playground equipment is old and unsafe. The church is responsible for determining if anything needs to be done to remedy the situation. In identifying risk, ask the safety officer to assess the problem and to submit a list of concerns. Here is his list of safety issues:

- The jungle gym sways when in use and is not appropriately secured to the ground.
- Chains on the swings have rusted.
- Wooden beams surrounding the fort reveal areas of numerous splinters.
- The tire swing has deteriorated, exposing steel bands.
- Protective ground cover is non-existent, exposing several rocks.
- Unsupervised children are playing in the dark during Bible study.
- The playground is not secured by a protective barrier to prevent unsupervised play during non-church hours.

Solutions may include dismantling the equipment and replacing it with newer and safer hardware. If the church decides to keep the current setup, it is obligated to promptly restore equipment to a safe condition. Here are a few things a church can do to address the previously listed concerns:

- Properly secure the jungle gym.
- Replace chains on the swing set.
- Sand and paint or stain wooden beams.
- Remove rocks and supply approved ground cover to cushion the earth.
- Always require adult supervision.

- Surround playground with a fence (I recommend coated chain link for visibility).
- Install a prominent sign outlining rules for playground use.
- Provide adequate lighting if the playground will be used at night.
- Require monthly inspections of the playground.

Are these safety measures reasonable to expect? You bet!

INSURANCE

Top 5 Reasons Churches Went to Court in 2017
(According to Church Law & Tax)

1. Sexual abuse of a child
2. Property disputes
3. Personal injuries
4. Zoning disputes
5. Insurance disputes

Church Lawsuits

- **2010:** A jury awarded $5 million to a minor against a church in the loss of his left foot due to a skiing accident on a church youth trip.
- **2015:** A Montana judge issued a $26 million insurance settlement in a quadriplegic man's lawsuit against a church as a result of an auto accident.
- **2019:** A lawsuit was filed — on behalf of a 3-year-old child — against a church in South Carolina where a volunteer was arrested for sexual abuse. The suit claims the church was negligent in training volunteers regarding sexual abuse, monitoring security cameras and following bathroom protocol for children.

The Bottom Line

Churches simply cannot self-fund these losses. Insurance is necessary, but so is a complete safety and security program working to protect the church.

Insurance Committee

Your congregational size and needs will determine the number of people who sit on this committee, but it is imperative that the church has someone watching over insurance concerns. Even in the smallest of churches, your insurance agent and an elder or church leader make the logical choice of people to comprise a basic committee. In churches of moderate to large size, the committee should be made up of the following people:

- Chairperson (insurance background preferred)
- Church's chief financial officer
- Church's safety representative
- Deacon, elder or another church leader
- Insurance agent

The committee will be responsible for the selection of an insurance company that understands the needs of a church. Although each church is different, here are some common insurance concerns:

- A building that is not used to its fullest except once or twice weekly
- Any property that is not adjacent to the main complex, such as multi-sites, a mission house or an office building
- Armed security
- Religious expression
- Malicious acts
- Travel for U.S. and foreign missions trips
- Sexual misconduct
- Church-owned vehicles
- Crime
- Key man coverage

- Nonprofit groups affiliated with the church (such as a bookstore, consignment shop, etc.)
- Workers' compensation claims

Review your coverage annually with updated documentation supplied by your agent. Use a video camera to document your assets. Work from the outside in. Start with parking lots and building exteriors and then move into classrooms and offices. Finally, make a video record of your office equipment, audio-visual gear, musical instruments, etc. Secure one copy off-site.

Church Vehicles

Ask your insurance company to provide motor vehicle records for everyone wishing to drive a church-owned vehicle. Some companies will do this at no charge. Your background screening company also possesses this capability. Each driver must meet the minimum requirements set forth by the church. There must be no exceptions. Here are a few important things to consider:

- All drivers must have a driver's license, be 21 years of age and possess a driving record that meets the church's guidelines.
- Run a Motor Vehicle Report on all qualified drivers at least once a year.
- Keep a fire extinguisher and first-aid kit in every vehicle.
- Place an accident information packet in each glove box. The bundle will contain emergency phone numbers, insurance company contact info and an accident form.
- Maintain each vehicle according to the owner's manual.
- Annually review your vehicle coverage with your insurance agent.
- Have one point of contact for all driver requests.

Occasionally, a van or pickup truck will be rented to transport an item that's too large for a passenger vehicle. Some insurance companies require rental drivers to be at least 25 years of age. The following page contains an example of driver guidelines.

EXAMPLE DRIVER GUIDELINES

An applicant must be at least [XX] years of age and submit a copy of his or her driver's license and insurance card to [approving person or department] at least one week before the intended use of the vehicle. This allows sufficient time to run a Motor Vehicle Records (MVR) check on the applicant. If the applicant is a foreign resident, he/she must have an approved international driver's license.

Approved drivers over the age of 65 should get an annual medical examination for hearing, eyesight, reflexes and general health. Each year, elderly drivers must submit a physician's statement to [approving person or department].

The applicant is **not** eligible to drive a [the name of your house of worship] vehicle if he/she has:

The following violations:

- ⊘ Vehicular homicide or assault
- ⊘ DUI / driving under the influence of alcohol or drugs
- ⊘ Open container or possession of a controlled substance in a vehicle
- ⊘ Conviction of a crime involving a motor vehicle
- ⊘ Leaving the scene of an accident/ hit and run
- ⊘ Eluding or attempting to elude a police officer
- ⊘ Reckless driving

Any one of the following violations that have occurred within the last three years:

- ⊘ Speeding 30 mph or more over the speed limit
- ⊘ Driving on the wrong side of the road
- ⊘ Racing

Any one of the following violations that have occurred within the last year:

- ⊘ Speeding more than 15 mph over the speed limit on a limited-access highway
- ⊘ Speeding more than 10 mph over the posted speed limit on any road other than a limited-access highway
- ⊘ Insurance cancellations or no liability insurance at all
- ⊘ Driving the wrong way on a one-way street
- ⊘ Two or more moving violations
- ⊘ An at-fault accident

Note: Some situations may require investigation and extra time to gather information to determine eligibility, such as a traffic accident. An authorized [person or department] must approve the request before the driver can use a vehicle. Yearly MVR checks will be run to ensure eligibility. It's the driver's responsibility to notify the [approving person or department] if he or she receives any citations or is convicted of any violation that may disqualify him or her.

Fifteen-Passenger Vans

Many houses of worship and private schools use 15-passenger vans to fill transportation needs. Most institutions own these vans but occasionally may rent one or more for mission trips or outings. Anyone with a driver's license is authorized to drive one. Often, you'll see one with luggage or camping gear strapped to the roof or towing a trailer.

Studies have shown that these vans can be unsafe. They are more prone to rollovers than other vehicles. The National Highway Traffic Safety Administration (NHTSA) says that from 1997 through 2006, these accidents accounted for more than 1,000 deaths, with about a third of these accidents occurring in the summer months. Moreover, victims were often ejected from the vehicle because they were not wearing seatbelts. Also, vans are not designed well to handle side-impact accidents. The NHTSA recommends that any vehicle carrying more than 10 passengers or transporting children meets federal school bus structural safety standards. If you are using 15-passenger vans, here are some recommendations:

- Create a safety training course that is required for all van drivers. Ask your insurance company for help.
- Have a certified defensive driving instructor teach a classroom course that covers skills applicable to the vans.
- Equip each van with a first-aid kit and fire extinguisher.
- Each driver must meet the minimum driver standards of your church and insurance company.
- Remove the rear seat. This helps to keep the center of gravity as far forward as possible.

- Fill the front seats with passengers first.
- All drivers and passengers must wear seatbelts. No exceptions.
- Require drivers to perform pre- and post-trip maintenance safety checks.
- Limit the number of riders to 12.
- Do not pull any trailers.
- Never load items on the roof.

Insurance companies suggest that churches should consider small shuttle buses instead of 15-passenger vans. These vehicles are designed to meet federal guidelines and are much safer than vans. The purchase price of a 15-passenger shuttle is higher than a van. However, in most cases, the additional cost will be recouped in reduced insurance rates. Keep in mind that some states are moving toward reclassifying 15-passenger vans as commercial vehicles. This would require drivers to have a commercial driver's license to drive them.

Safety While Traveling in a Vehicle

Have you ever read or heard stories of good Samaritans? Some of these stories tug on your heart and motivate you to help the less fortunate. You feel like getting in your car to cruise the streets at 2 a.m., looking for someone to help. OK, maybe not.

I'm not against giving aid when aid is needed, or even giving my time to help an organization that improves people's lives. God will lead us to do remarkable things in His name. But before you act, I would like you to think and act responsibly. Share these true stories with your staff and volunteers to avoid getting in trouble.

A CLOSE CALL

I have a friend who is a law enforcement officer and drives an unmarked unit. On his way to church one evening, he came across a disabled vehicle on the interstate. The hood of the vehicle was up, and there appeared to be a family in the car. They had parked on the shoulder of the road, so my friend stopped to help. Pulling up behind the vehicle, he activated his flashing police grille and window lights and walked up to the car.

The four people — a husband, wife and two children — told him that they had run out of gas. He offered to get gas for them, asking if the teenage boy or dad wanted to come along. They both refused and said they would wait with the family. He drove to the next exit, — about a mile away — borrowed a gas can from the gas station, and returned.

When he returned, the car was gone. Could they have gotten gas from someone else? Possibly. However, he feels otherwise. He believes that they were parked there prepared to commit a crime. Maybe it was to solicit money from an unsuspecting good Samaritan — or worse, to commit a robbery. My friend feels that if it wasn't for his flashing lights, he might have been a victim.

WHEN RIGHT TURNS WRONG

A church member was returning home from an out-of-state work assignment. It was after midnight on a lonely stretch of the interstate when he noticed a car on the shoulder with its hood up. He counted three heads and decided to stop and help. He pulled up on the shoulder and got out, offering assistance.

As he walked up to the car, three men got out and met him. When he was close, one of the men punched him in the face. He fell into a ditch next to the car, stunned. They began to yell at him and told him to empty his pockets. They took everything: keys, money, a wallet and his cellphone. As he lay on the ground, reeling from the attack, they told him not to move or they would kill him. They said someone would be watching him for the next few hours. He lay in the cold, dark ditch feeling sick as they drove off in both cars.

Although he didn't realize it at the time, God protected him. In an instant, the situation could have gone from bad to worse. Many of these crimes result in the murder of the victim. The moral of the story is to resist the urge to stop. Instead, call 911 to direct assistance to the disabled vehicle.

PROTECTED BY

BRICKHOUSE
S E C U R I T Y

24 HR Monitoring
Offsite Recording

But whoever listens to me will live in safety and be at ease, without fear of harm.

PROVERBS 1:33 (NIV)

According to the U.S. Fire Administration, 30 percent of church fires are the result of mechanical failures. Faulty wiring and improperly functioning heating systems are often at fault, perhaps because they are in older structures and have not been brought up to local fire codes. Of churches that reported fires, 96 percent had no sprinkler system. Kitchen and cooking area fires accounted for 23 percent of church fires.

Are you ready to get started? Form a safety committee. If the size of your church doesn't warrant an entire committee to handle safety, appoint a safety officer. A committee should include volunteer safety experts such as a building inspector, a corporate safety director or a government safety official. Retired persons, including police officers, function well on the committee. An appointed or elected church official (deacon or elder) oversees the group and provides spiritual guidance.

In a smaller church, the safety officer solicits information from various government agencies, safety organizations and associations for help in determining job descriptions, duties and goals of the committee. Building and grounds inspections are the primary responsibilities of a safety committee or a safety officer. Following a careful examination of the facility, the committee or officer makes recommendations to reduce the risks of any hazards they may have discovered during the inspections.

Hold initial meetings at least once a quarter and keep all documentation on file with the chairperson. He or she will send a copy to the insurance committee and the insurance agent. Less frequent meetings are needed as you resolve your list of concerns. During site inspections, the group should use a Risk Management Checklist that covers fire prevention and protection, first aid, floor safety, lighting, etc. Ask your insurance agent for a checklist.

I recommend that your safety officer meets with the local fire marshal, fire inspector or fire chief. Request that he or she visits your facility to make suggestions on making your building(s) safer. Their advice is invaluable and free. Your insurance agent should meet with the committee and inspect your house of worship once a year.

FIRE SAFETY
Inspections

Inspect fire safety items annually. If a complex or a building is more than 20 years old, inspect it at least every six months. Details on an inspection list include but are not limited to:

- Fire extinguishers must be inspected monthly by the safety officer or a designated volunteer/staff member. An approved fire safety company must perform a yearly inspection and attach new tags.
  - If sprinklers cover your entire building, your local fire department may not require you to hang any fire extinguishers. Even in this situation, you may want to have a few in critical areas, such as in your kitchen and maintenance areas.
- Sprinkler system (if the building is so equipped).
- Fire suppression systems (kitchen hoods and computer rooms).
  - These systems typically need to be inspected every six months.
- Batteries on fire exit signs and emergency lighting.
  - Most exit signs and emergency lighting fixtures have an attached battery. These batteries have a life of between one and five years. Newer buildings have emergency devices hard wired into an electrical panel or a larger battery in an electrical closet. This is more cost-effective.

- Check to see that all flammable liquids and materials are properly stored in a safety storage cabinet.
- Storage closets need to be organized and maintained.
- Do not use mechanical rooms as storage areas.
- Do not padlock, chain or block fire exit doors.
- Change batteries in smoke detectors every six months.
- Install carbon monoxide detectors in kitchens and areas utilizing natural gas burners.

Fire-Retardant Material

Ideally, use only fire-retardant materials inside your complex. This includes furniture, lampshades, curtains and decorations. When using hay or straw for a Christmas pageant, spray it with flame retardant to reduce the chance of fire. If you build a temporary set for your Easter or Christmas pageant, use fire-retardant-treated wood. **CAUTION: Fire-treated wood loses its durability over time. If you plan to use building materials year after year, use metal studs and supports instead of wood.**

Make sure participants who carry lighted torches have a small fire extinguisher under the costumes. Alternatively, have an attendant carry an extinguisher in a bag or under his or her garb while walking alongside participants with torches.

Candles

If your church serves as a wedding venue, you will have requests to burn candles. Use no-drip wedding candles for such occasions to reduce the chance of a fire. Stage a small fire extinguisher within a few feet of the burning candles, just in case of an unexpected incident. Make sure the minister and wedding coordinator know where it is and how to operate it. Place the extinguisher out of sight behind plants or somewhere on stage.

Staff members, teenagers and Bible study groups may want to burn candles to create a particular atmosphere in a classroom or office. First, check with the Fire Marshal to see if candles are permitted anywhere in the building. If so, a good general rule is to keep all open flames encased in a surrounding glass container like a hurricane chimney. Be sure the glass container is taller than the flame produced by the candle. Some people adhere to the premise that "it's easier to ask for forgiveness than to get permission in advance." Do not apply such a principle when dealing with government officials. You want to create mutual trust and respect with authorities to ensure a good working relationship.

Fire Escape Plan

Have a fire evacuation plan. Work with the local fire department or Fire Marshal to determine the specific needs for your facility. More and more, fire departments load floor plans of commercial buildings into iPads to use when responding to an alarm. Check with your fire department to see if this is available. When forming your fire escape plan, consider the following:

- What do you do if a fire alarm sounds during worship service?
  - In smaller churches, evacuate the building. The children's ministry should have a designated place outside of the building where parents can meet their children.
  - In larger churches, the same rule applies. Evacuate. Some churches have segregated alarms, meaning that if one area is in alarm, another is not. Evacuate the area that is in alarm. Evacuate to the outside of the building or an area that is not in alarm. Have the Fire Marshal and your fire alarm monitoring company approve this fire evacuation plan.
- What is the safest way to evacuate disabled participants?
  - As soon as the alarm sounds, an usher or greeter should get to the person in the wheelchair. Wait until the bulk of the crowd leaves the worship center and accompany the disabled person to a safe area. Waiting until the crowd clears prevents possible injury when others rush to get out.
  - A large church may have multiple floors serviced by elevators. Do not use elevators for evacuation. If the disabled person is on an upper level, you may need to ask for help to get them down a flight of stairs. Some buildings have stairwells with concrete walls. A safe short-term solution may be to go to a stairwell for safety and remain there. Text or call someone to let them know where you are. If there is an actual fire in the vicinity, you may need to ask for assistance to carry the person to safety.
- Issue a copy of the fire plan in a condensed version to all staff and volunteers.

- Have a diagram of the emergency escape route(s) posted on the inside wall next to an exit door in rooms that seat 50 or more people.

- Designate ushers.

  ○ In small churches, ushers should direct people out of the building by pointing to the nearest exit. In larger churches where you may have multiple floors and exits, post ushers at each door on every level. Also assign ushers to seating sections, to direct people to a specific exit. This will prevent overcrowding at points of egress.

- Train staff and key volunteers on the details of your evacuation plan.

  ○ Designate a weekend as a safety weekend. Outline the evacuation plan, including guidelines regarding picking up children, in an insert in your bulletin. Hold quarterly practice drills for the children's area. Remember to monitor how long it takes to vacate the building and look for areas that require improvement.

OTHER EMERGENCIES
Severe-Weather Plan

Severe weather can be — and often is — more devastating than fire. Tornadoes, harsh wind, hail and flooding can wreak havoc not only on facilities but also to services and activities going on at church. Check with your insurance agent/broker to determine what coverage you have over weather-related problems. Regular property and casualty insurance does not generally cover flooding. You may need a separate policy for flood coverage.

Ask the builder or architect to recommend shelter areas in your complex. If the facility is old, the local building inspector may help. The general rule is to get to the center of the lowest level of the building. In newer buildings with poured concrete stairwells, the stairwells serve as excellent safe areas. During non-service hours, the staff and visitors should gather in the stairways for safety. During a service, make it a priority to direct people to safety without causing panic. Parents will naturally be concerned about their children, so make sure parents always know where the children are. Sign up for weather alerts from your local authorities and media outlets on your cellphone.

Weather terms used by the local media to identify storm systems:

- **Tornado Watch:** Tornadoes are likely. Be ready to take shelter.
- **Tornado Warning:** A tornado has been sighted or is indicated by radar. Take shelter immediately.
- **Winter Storm Watch:** Severe winter weather is possible. Listen for updates.
- **Winter Storm Warning:** Severe winter weather is expected. Find out when the storm is expected and take precautions.
- **Blizzard Warning:** Severe winter weather with sustained winds of at least 35 miles per hour is expected.
- **Traveler's Advisory:** Severe winter conditions may make driving difficult or dangerous.

Earthquakes

Earthquakes occur most frequently west of the Rocky Mountains, although historically the most violent earthquakes have occurred in the central United States. Earthquakes occur suddenly and without warning.

- If indoors, stay there. Take cover under a sturdy piece of furniture or a counter. If you don't have time to get under furniture, brace yourself against an inside wall or stand under a door frame. Protect your head and neck.
- If outdoors, move away from buildings, streetlights and utility lines.
- Do not use elevators during and after an earthquake.
- After an earthquake, stay away from windows and items that could fall.
- If you are close to the ocean and the quake is strong enough to knock you down, head for higher ground immediately. Earthquakes that are centered close to a shoreline are likely to cause a tidal wave, also known as a tsunami. Depending on the location of the quake, the wave may hit shore immediately or up to 15 minutes later. It's not the height of the wave that can kill you but the speed of it. A typical wave is no more than 3 or 4 feet high when traveling in the ocean. However, it moves at hundreds of miles per hour, picking up debris at the shoreline and causing destruction and death.

MAINTENANCE CONSIDERATIONS

Many of our houses of worship have maintenance departments. This department may consist of only one staff member or volunteer, but safety guidelines must be in place.

- Have a first-aid kit and eyewash station available in the work area.
- Properly train anyone using equipment or chemicals on proper use and emergency procedures.
- Keep records of all training.
- Have a lock-out/tag-out kit available.
- Properly store any chemicals, paints, solvents or used rags in fire cabinets or containers.
- Keep safety data sheets, material safety data sheets or product safety data sheets on hand for all chemicals, including ordinary household products. Instruct staff and volunteers on their location and use.
- Create a preventative maintenance (PM) log for items such as plumbing, wiring, gas lines, major appliances, lights, etc. Follow the manufacturers' recommended inspection intervals.
- Post an emergency contact list including:
  - Key staff and volunteers
  - Electrician
  - Plumber
  - Locksmith
  - Animal removal expert

EXAMPLE BAPTISTRY TRAGEDY

In 2005, a minister entered a baptistry to conduct a baptism. Unknown at the time, the water heater for the baptistry was malfunctioning and placing 80 volts of electricity through the water. The minister was electrocuted when he stepped on a metal drain and grabbed a wired microphone. All efforts to revive him failed.

Lessons learned from this tragedy: Never use a wired microphone in the baptistry. Always use a wireless unit. Replace the metal drain cover with a plastic drain cover. Conduct scheduled inspections of electrical components including the pump, filter and heater. A licensed electrician must perform these inspections.

Lighting

Interior lighting includes night lights when the building is closed and sufficient lighting when the building is in use. Motion lights work well inside entryways to prevent anyone from trying to break in through a door or window. These lights look like emergency lighting and come in different-colored housings to match interior walls. Can someone be seen from the outside when he or she is working late? Mini-blinds or curtains provide a degree of privacy and safety from someone who may be lurking outside.

White LED lights work better than sodium or low-sodium lighting for exteriors and parking lots. White light permits you to distinguish colors. Sodium only reveals different shades of gray. It is also harder to hide under white light. If you're illuminating your structure, remember to point some light to the ground surrounding the building to prevent hiding spots.

Keep the parking lot lights on until all vehicles have left. Keep a few on for night lighting. Install motion sensor lights at the corners of buildings — high enough not to be tampered with but low enough to provide sufficient coverage.

Locks, Keys and Access Control

- Use "Grade 1" hardware as a minimum requirement for keys. It is a good idea to use restricted key access for exterior doors. This controls duplication by requiring a signature before the authorized locksmith can make a duplicate key.

- Restrict key authorization to two people. One person will be the primary contact and the other will be a backup. Have a key log and require signatures for every key issued. Several security firms offer user-friendly and efficient key-tracking software.

- Issue keys only to staff and a few trusted volunteers.

- You may also protect high-traffic areas with an electronic or mechanical stand-alone keypad. These keypads can also protect sensitive or private sectors.

- Churches of all sizes use electronic access control. It's becoming more affordable and easier to use. A simple system might include all exterior doors and a few sensitive areas, such as the computer room and the senior pastor's office. These are tied to a single computer with a server that reads staff member ID cards, allowing entry at authorized times. For instance, some people would be allowed 24-hour access, while others would be limited to regular office hours. These cards and fobs come in many different styles, incorporating magnetic stripes, bar codes or hidden wires/computer chips (proximity). They can also include a photo ID printed on them. Many people prefer the key fob because of its size, but a photo ID has advantages in a large church where the staff is required to wear an ID. I like the proximity cards over the magnetic stripes and barcodes, which have been known to fade over time and make entry difficult.

- Biometric readers have replaced some card access systems. The three-dimensional hand readers in manufacturing facilities allow employees to clock in and clock out, but this system is too cumbersome to work in a church setting. Fingerprint identification can be used as a secondary requirement for computer login, but current functionality is unreliable. Please do not consider it as a primary source for security access control at this point.

SECURITY EQUIPMENT
Alarms

- Electronic alarms are generally a good investment. However, your building size and layout will determine your requirements and how best to utilize alarm components.

- Some megachurches have no electronic alarms. The size would not make it economical. In most cases, these churches have 24-hour security services on premises. In this application, an alarm could still be used to protect a computer room or a room containing the church's safe.

- Consult with at least three alarm companies for bids on an alarm system. Check within your congregation first for someone who might be in the business. Contact a local company, then contact at least two national companies. National does not always mean better, but it will offer some comparison before you make your decision. If you are a novice in this area, ask a lot of questions when they visit. After three visits, you'll have a pretty good understanding of what you need and what they can do for you.

- The system should include coverage for all exterior entry points. Every door and window need not have contacts. An interior motion alarm sensor can cover a broad area. It should also feature a perimeter-only setting. This allows someone to work within the building, yet have exterior entry points armed.

- If you have an alarm system, equip your essential personnel such as the senior minister, his administrative assistant and the receptionist with a silent distress device. These devices are small, portable and can be kept on a desk or in a drawer. When operated, they immediately send a silent alarm to your monitoring company. The police will respond as if there is an emergency on your premises. Be prepared for their armed entrance.

- In May 2007, in a town in New York, surveillance video of a woman warding off an attacker with a pen led to the arrest of a 44-year-old man. The woman was praying early Wednesday morning when she fought off the attacker by stabbing him in the neck with a pen she was using to write in her journal. The man ran off. The church's security cameras recorded the attack. The suspect was arrested Thursday evening after an off-duty firefighter spotted him riding a bike. He recognized the suspect from local news coverage.

- Police released surveillance video of two masked men who allegedly robbed one of the oldest churches in Dallas on Thanksgiving Day 2007. The men tied up three workers at the church in downtown Dallas. A video shows them stealing flat-screen TVs worth thousands of dollars. Investigators said the men wore black fatigues and carried semi-automatic pistols. Police said, "The odd thing about this is that it's a very professional robbery. Wearing black fatigues and things such as that, you don't see that a lot." The masked men confronted a female security guard, bound her and dragged her into a closet. They also tied up and locked two other security guards and placed them in separate closets. The guards spent more than two hours locked up until one of them worked himself free and called the police. A security camera caught the suspects leaving in a silver Dodge Dakota pickup. A day after the robbery, police arrested a 26-year-old man and charged him with aggravated robbery.

- In April 2016, a female fitness instructor was scheduled to lead a 5 a.m. class inside a Midlothian, Texas, church. Church security video shows her arriving at about 4:15 a.m. Shortly before 5 a.m., one of her students found her dead inside the church. Security footage revealed a suspect walking in the church around 4:30 a.m. The suspect was wearing police SWAT tactical gear and carrying a hammer, smashing glass and breaking doors as he/she walked around. The murder occurred in an area where there was no security camera coverage. The suspect is still at large.

- In 2018, an adult male volunteer in a Charleston, South Carolina, church was arrested and charged with 14 counts of child sexual abuse. The original abuse report led police to watch camera footage from the previous 90 days, as that was as long as the security system archived footage. They charged the suspect with an additional 13 counts of abuse. The report indicates that the abuse occurred in a bathroom attached to the classroom. The bathroom had "Dutch" or half-doors. The top half of the door always remained open in clear view of the classroom's security camera. Even with the bottom half of the door closed, video shows the suspect abusing the children. A lawsuit was filed on behalf of the children. The lawsuit claims that there was live feedback to a security monitor where a volunteer was supposedly assigned to watch it; however, the abuse was not reported immediately to the police.

Security Cameras

Security cameras are a tremendous asset when used correctly — as a deterrent, for evidence-gathering and in some cases, as a crime-stopping tool. Technology advances quickly, and new cameras and systems frequently hit the market. The question is: What's best for you? I'll provide you with the necessary information to help you make that decision, but always seek professional advice.

- **Where to Start:** If you're new to this and do not have a system, install and grow it incrementally. You could start with a four-camera system, then add more cameras as funds become available. If you have an electrician and/or someone that works in IT, you can install the system with their help. Otherwise, almost all alarm companies can install cameras for you.

- **Placing the Cameras:** Start with all exterior doors. Place the camera on the inside with a view of the entire entrance. You want a good picture of people coming in and going out. Do not place the camera too high in a corner. If you make this mistake, the only view you will get is of someone's hat, not his or her face. Next, move into the money room, interior hallways, gathering spaces, children's classrooms, adult classrooms, general office space and parking lots. It is against the law to record areas such as restrooms and adult lockers or changing areas.

- **Cost:** I've seen a complete 12-camera IP system with a digital recorder for less than $800 at a big box retailer. Factors such as cameras, the type of digital storage chosen, the amount of digital storage, wiring, installation and other features drive the cost of a camera system. Cameras will range from $125 to more than $3,000 each. I've installed a few indoor $125 cameras with great results. Some of them are still operating 15 years later. Seek out and visit end users for references on cameras and systems. A business the same size as your campus is an excellent place to start. Colleges, universities and hospitals may also provide valuable feedback. Although they are large, much of what they tell you will be invaluable. Ask what companies they've used and whom they would recommend.

- **Internet Protocol (IP) vs. Hard-Wired Cameras:** IP cameras are wireless digital video cameras that can send and receive data via a computer network and the internet. The video is transmitted over the air to a receiver that records the video. A wired camera sends video over a hardwired connection to a receiver. Wireless (IP) cameras have been known to lose a signal and drop the link to the receiver, but industry experts say that technology has improved and with the right installation, it rarely happens. Wireless cameras are also easier to install, only needing to be close to a power source. Wireless cameras require the inclusion of your IT staff. Bandwidth, configurations, server and storage space are a few considerations necessary to run the system. A wired network will need minimal support from IT to set up remote access by PC, smartphone or other devices. Of course, wired cameras will cost more to install.

- **PTZ or Fixed:** Pan-tilt-zoom (PTZ) cameras are more expensive than fixed cameras. Fixed cameras work well in classrooms, hallways and building entrances and can be programmed to record only when they detect movement in the field of vision. PTZ cameras work best in your worship center, other large gathering spaces and parking lots. You can configure PTZ cameras to conduct a programmed panning patrol. Consider that a PTZ camera on patrol will require more storage space as it is continuously moving.

- **Recording Video:** Network Video Recorders (NVRs) and Digital Video Recorders (DVRs) are hardware used to store and manage your video. DVRs are usually attached to an existing wired system using older analog cameras that need the video files converted to digital formats. You may add newer wired cameras to the system. NVRs handle both wired and wireless (IP) cameras. Consider that DVRs and NVRs work best with cameras from compatible manufacturers. Ask before you buy. Storage space for recording is only limited by how much you are willing to spend. Many DVRs and NVRs come with built-in large-capacity hard drives. You can order the amount of space in the unit — such as 2 or 3 terabytes — and still install an external hard drive for more space. Additional space is essential when you are trying to add days to the recording time. Most systems are usually set to record for 20 to 30 days. The example at the start of the chapter where the church archived 90 days of footage is rare. However, it proved worthwhile in the arrest of the perpetrator.

● What Must My System Do?

- ○ Stay on 24/7, with the capability to command activation, such as record on motion, send an alarm or operate on a schedule
- ○ Able to quickly retrieve and duplicate video for external use
- ○ Have clear day and night vision
- ○ Allow remote viewing of live and recorded video through PC and mobile devices
- ○ Have strong support from the vendor

Bullet-Resistant Glass

The Underwriters Laboratory (UL) — the primary testing organization — establishes eight levels of bullet-resistant glass. I suggest looking at Level 1 and 2. Or even Level 3 for heightened protection. Level 1 protection is the least expensive of the levels. Level 8 is the most costly. Level 1 may not stop a bullet from a high-powered gun, but the coating will keep the glass intact and not allow the intruder easy access into your building. Suppliers and independent contractors have formed partnerships across the country, so it will be reasonably easy to find an installer in your area.

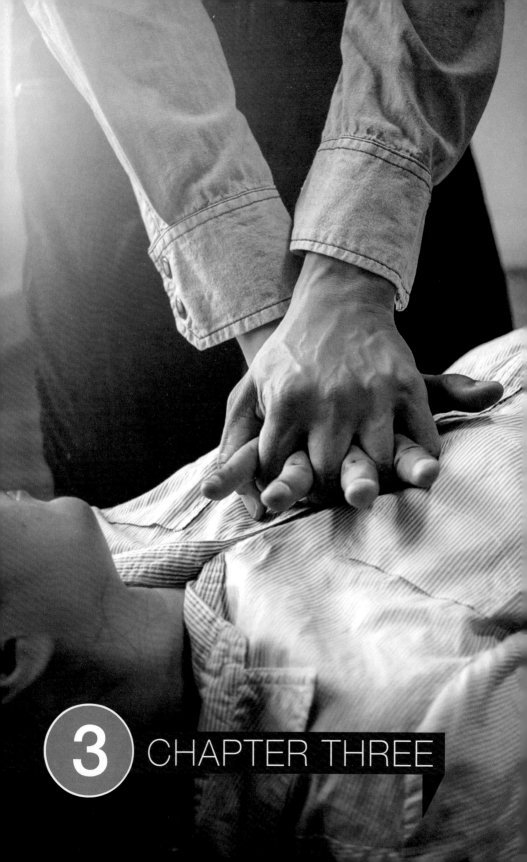

3 CHAPTER THREE

MEDICAL PROGRAM

- Readiness
- Response
- Event Planning
- Recreation
- Actual Medical Incidents

...I was sick and you looked after me...

MATTHEW 25:36 (NIV)

READINESS

It's a glorious Sunday morning. You're sitting in church with fellow worshippers. The pastor is delivering a powerful message. Suddenly you hear a scream and see a commotion in the middle of the worship center. Someone has collapsed, and others are yelling for help. You're hoping there's a doctor in the crowd. You wonder if someone is calling an ambulance. If this were to happen in your church, would you be prepared? It's not a question of if this is going to happen. It's a question of when this will happen. Your preparedness may save a life. How do you start?

- **Seek counsel.** Ask your attorney and insurance agent about the use of medical professionals for a volunteer medical team. The good Samaritan law in your state should protect their treatment of someone in distress. Learn about guidelines limiting treatment using a first-aid kit, oxygen and an Automated External Defibrillator (AED).

- **Put someone in charge.** Find a medical professional in your congregation who will accept the responsibility of organizing your medical response team. In a smaller church, that team may consist of only that professional. In larger churches, that group will include doctors, nurses, EMTs and paramedics. I find that these professionals usually work odd shifts, which do not allow them to volunteer in other ministries. Given the opportunity, many would like to give something back to their church by helping on the team. The goal is to have medical assistance at every service and large event.

- **Do background checks.** Your medical team will be working with patients of all ages. Treat them like children's volunteers and run them through your clearance protocol for children. This would include a national criminal background check as well as a national sex offender registry search.

- **Designate a first-aid room.** The room should be easily accessible from the worship area. Locate the first-aid room on the first floor to avoid the need to use stairs. The exit door should be wide enough to accommodate an EMS stretcher. Also, the room should have a sink, be well lit and have a tile floor. Setting aside a place specifically for first-aid is difficult for some churches. If your church is in this situation, consider alternatives. The room is going to be used rarely and only for short periods. I know of a church that uses the men's restroom adjacent to the worship center. They have a wheelchair and stretcher stored in a closet close by and an usher or greeter is tasked with clearing the bathroom of people and retrieving the wheelchair and stretcher. A sturdy 4-foot by 8-foot table can be brought in to act as an examination table.

● Contents of Medical Bag Taken to Scene

- ○ Stethoscope
- ○ Blood pressure equipment
- ○ Nitrile gloves
- ○ Glucose
- ○ Flashlight
- ○ Band-aids
- ○ Gauze
- ○ Tourniquet

● First-Aid Room Equipment:

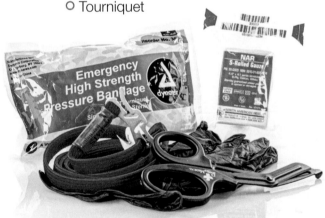

- ○ Commercial-sized first-aid kit
- ○ AED
- ○ Examination table
- ○ Portable oxygen
- ○ Wheelchair
- ○ Bleeding control kit: The military developed these kits. They are now popular first-aid items for schools, universities and arenas across the country. I would recommend speaking to your local EMS to determine what will work for you and where to get training. The kits are now available online at most large retailers and through local medical supply companies.

RESPONSE

During a training session at the house of worship, the medical team will make the determination where to render medical assistance. In most cases, I recommend removing the patient to the first-aid room to cause the least disruption to the service and to provide privacy for the patient. Smaller venues are more likely to experience disruption. The pastor or worship leader should immediately get up and ask the congregation to pray for the patient and the people attending to him or her. Having everyone stand allows the medical staff to work without onlookers. In a large church, if the patient can't be moved promptly, the same protocol applies. If more time is needed, singing a song may also be appropriate.

During service, the general recommendation is to remove the patient from the public worship area to an outside hallway, then to the first-aid room. In more severe cases, such as a cardiac arrest where CPR or other life-saving procedures are required, bring a stretcher or a wheelchair along with the medical bag to the scene.

The medical person in charge has full responsibility for treatment. He or she will determine if the patient may be released or if EMS needs to be called. Usually, once EMS arrives, they assume responsibility for the care and transport of the patient to a medical center.

Support Staff

The medical team may require assistance in crowd control, notification of EMS, locating family members and obtaining first-aid equipment. Ushers and security team members can assist the team as requested. If the emergency occurs when traffic is heavy in your parking lots, traffic control may be needed to allow EMS to enter and leave the property.

Assignment

Unless you have a very small congregation, I recommend that you have at least two medical volunteers working at each service. Most emergencies are best handled by at least two professionals. Team members should also watch over the children's department.

Communication / Two-Way Radios

Over the years, after trying everything from pagers to cellphones to cellphone apps, I've found that two-way radios work best. You want clear, instantaneous back-and-forth communication that can target an individual or a group.

Two-way radios equipped with earpieces allow the medical and security teams to stay in contact with one another, as well as to call for assistance while sitting in services without disrupting fellow worshipers. High-end family channel radios have multiple channels with earpiece capability. Available at most department and electronics stores, the radios sell for $20 to $80 apiece. Be sure to purchase rechargeable radios. I also recommend issuing radios to head ushers, greeters, parking lot attendants and supervisors in your children's department.

Larger facilities may want to look for more sophisticated "business band" or commercial UHF radios that have 3 to 5 watts of power. UHF stands for Ultra High Frequency. These radios work well inside buildings. You may hear about VHF radios, but they work best outside. Vast complexes may require a repeater that boosts the radio signal. You can have multiple repeaters, each assigned to a specific channel.

These commercial radios are usually purchased from a professional communications business. The provider can also help submit your application for and assign an FCC radio license for your location. The license allows the use of multiple channels on multiple radios with no outside interference and eavesdropping. The permit currently costs $500 and it keeps your license in force for 10 years. Have your radio supplier visit your location and run tests to see what radios work best.

In large churches with multiple channels for security, medical, children's, ushers, traffic, etc., a volunteer dispatcher should monitor the main channels. Provide them with access to a phone in case EMS or law enforcement is needed.

Usually, the security lead will have the responsibility to make assignments and send security or medical team members to the scene of an emergency. If an usher sees a medical emergency, he calls the security lead who then dispatches the medical team. Security notification prevents a heightened security response to a medical incident.

Documentation

You must have a confidential incident form that contains information gathered from the patient and the attending medical team member. If the injury occurred on your property, you could face a civil lawsuit. A well-documented incident form may be useful in court. The form should contain the following information:

- Name of person filling out the report
- Patient's name, address, home number, gender and date of birth
- Location of incident
- Witnesses' names, addresses and phone numbers
- Synopsis of the incident
- What treatment did the team administer?
- Who administered treatment?
- Was EMS called?
- Time EMS was called and time they arrived
- Was the patient released or taken to a medical facility?
- Parents' names (if a juvenile)
- Parents' time of notification

Follow-Up

Call the patient or the patient's family within 24 hours to check on how he or she is doing. If the patient was taken to a hospital, notify your hospital visitation ministry.

EVENT PLANNING

Occasionally, your church will have the opportunity to host an event that will attract a large crowd. Maybe it's an Easter pageant or a Christmas special. Churches have found that it makes good sense to pay to have an ambulance and its crew on site during the event. The added medical assistance quickly affords life support and other emergency functions by working alongside your medical team. Check with your local EMS provider for availability. Most areas have government-owned ambulances and private EMS providers. Private contractors are more likely to work for an hourly contract fee. EMS providers will have two levels of care vehicles. The first is Basic Life Support (BLS) and the second is Advanced Life Support (ALS). Talk to your provider to determine which best suits your needs.

While on a church-sponsored hike in a wilderness area, a teenage boy fell into a ravine and injured his back. As a precaution, he was not moved until a rescue squad arrived from the local fire department. Because of the remote location, he was taken to a hospital by a medical helicopter. The media picked up the story and arrived at the staging area with the fire department. The story was front-page news the next morning.

People may get hurt while participating in a recreational activity that is sponsored by the church, whether on church property or not. The responsibility of the church is to try to prevent any injuries through supervision and training of leaders, as well as by providing details and instructions to participants. Consider the following recommendations:

- Maintain updated signed release forms on all participants.
- Keep a current list of participants.
- Have completed medical releases with emergency contacts on file for each person.
- Ensure authorized adults supervise activities.
- Inspect and maintain equipment.
- Train adult leaders on the proper use of equipment.
- Have emergency procedures in place (cellphones, emergency contact list, first-aid kit, etc.)
- Certify all leaders in first aid, CPR, AED use and control of bleeding.

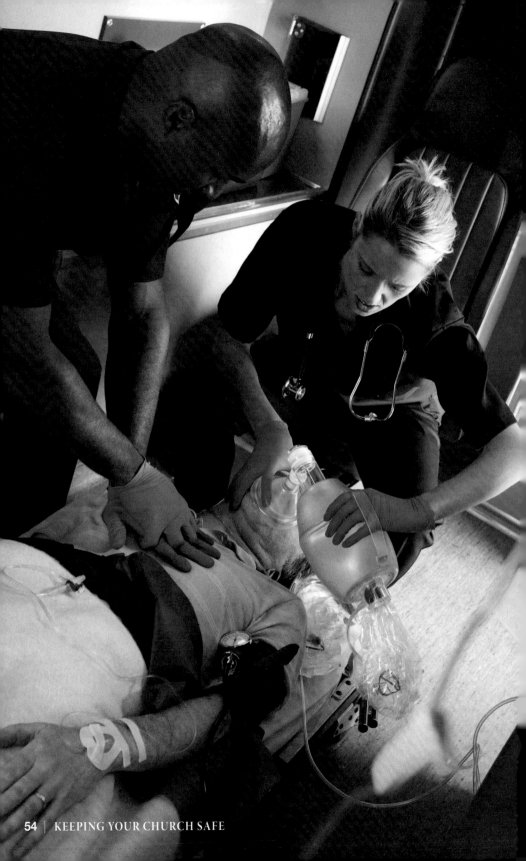

- During a five-hour, community family fun day at a church, there were 15 calls for minor medical assistance and one transport by EMS to a hospital. Most injuries were from minors using bounce houses and sizable inflatable water slides.

- A senior man collapsed while playing basketball. An AED used by a staff member saved his life.

- While attending an event, a senior woman suffered a cardiac arrest. All efforts to revive her failed.

- An out-of-town visitor felt tightness in her chest and numbness in her arm. EMS arrived, but she refused to leave, saying she was OK. Upon insistence from the medical team, she was transported and had a triple bypass the next day.

- During a softball game on the church's field, a man playing catcher had his nose broken from a tipped foul ball.

- A woman walking into church caught her shoe's heel on the sidewalk, fell and fractured her wrist.

- An actor had a horse step on his foot while performing in an Easter pageant.

- An actress portraying Mary fell off a donkey during a church play.

- A tech crew member was overcome by toxic fumes while trying to put out a fire originating from a set piece on stage.

4 CHAPTER FOUR

- Mail Bombs
- Not So Funny
- Identifying a Suspicious Package
- Biological Agents

I call to the Lord, who is worthy of praise, and I am saved from my enemies.

2 SAMUEL 22:4 (NIV)

MAIL BOMBS

U.S. Mail delivered a box about the size of a large cake box to a church. The package was addressed to "Senior Pastor" and had no return address. The address was handwritten on the white box. The postmark indicated the package originated from within the same city as the church. The senior pastor's administrative assistant opened the box to discover an unsigned card with handwritten scripture written on it. The box also contained a stuffed rooster, about 14 inches tall. She put the rooster back in the box and closed it. A staff member took the box to a classroom and opened it. While doing this, he heard a ticking sound. When he noticed the rooster, he immediately vacated the area, thinking it was a bomb. Investigators arrived and found no bomb. The ticking noise was coming from a wall clock above the counter where the staff member had opened the box for inspection.

Although this story is somewhat humorous and has a good ending, it highlights the need to be well informed and trained in how to handle suspicious packages. Contact the Bureau of Alcohol, Tobacco, Firearms and Explosives (ATF) for information and training on how to handle suspicious mail and packages.

EXAMPLE NOT SO FUNNY

Here are two stories that were much more serious than the first example in this chapter:

- In 1999, a mail bomb intended for a Texas televangelist exploded prematurely at a U.S. Postal Service bulk mail center in Dallas. The package containing the pipe bomb was on a conveyor belt about 20 feet above the floor when it exploded. No one was injured. An arrest was made in Las Vegas after a man telephoned a mental health facility saying that he was planning to use explosives.

- October 2018: A Florida man was arrested and charged with mailing 14 pipe bombs to prominent Democratic politicians as well as critics of President Trump. Authorities said he had a list of about 100 possible targets.

IDENTIFYING A SUSPICIOUS PACKAGE

- No return address
- Restrictive markings such as, "Personal," "XX's Eyes Only," "Confidential," etc.
- Excessive postage
- Mailed from a foreign country and not expected
- Misspelled words in the address
- Addressed to a title or a person only or having an incorrect title
- Badly typed or written
- Protruding wires
- Lopsided or uneven
- Rigid or bulky
- Excessive tape or string
- The postmark does not match the return address

BIOLOGICAL AGENTS

The anthrax virus has been the most common form of biological exposure in the United States. The virus has been attached to a powdery substance in letters and packages, then sent through the U.S. Mail. Many cases were reported shortly after the 9/11 attack. Some cases were confirmed, but many were false. Reported cases have diminished dramatically since 2005. Mailrooms across the country implemented stringent mail handling procedures. However, since the number of reported cases has dropped, complacency has settled in, and many of us are back to doing business as we did "pre-9/11."

You may not want to implement stringent measures unless authorities have raised the threat level or a direct threat is made against churches in general or your house of worship directly. I do, however, recommend necessary precautions, especially in identifying suspicious packages. Anyone handling mail should be familiar with these best practices.

Anthrax exposes itself three ways: cutaneous (through the skin), inhalational and gastrointestinal. Confirmed criminal cases have involved the cutaneous and inhalational types. Anthrax organisms can cause infection to the skin, digestive system or lungs. To do so, the organism must be rubbed into the skin, swallowed or inhaled as a fine aerosolized mist. An infected person develops flu-like symptoms, which become severe. Black ulcers may appear on the skin that was exposed. In most cases, treatment with the appropriate antibiotics can arrest the disease. Anthrax does not spread from one person to another person.

Additional Identifiers

- Makes a sandy noise or any other noise when moved
- Strange odor or chemical smell
- Leaking any fluid
- Oily stains or discolorations on the outer packaging
- Crystallization on wrapper

Guidelines

- Use disposable medical or rubber gloves to open mail.
- Hold the envelope up to a light; look for powder or sand-like substance before opening.

- Open mail on a designated table, not on your desk.
- Open mail over a large rubber or plastic tub that can be sealed with a lid.
- Use an opener and do not use the opener for anything else.
- Open envelopes from the bottom.
- When opening, preserve the return address, postmarks and any other writings that are visible.
- Do not have any desk or ceiling fans running and do not open mail next to an open window.
- Don't shake, pound or tamper with suspicious mail.
- Seal any suspicious mail in a clear zip-close bag.
- If you find a suspected envelope, leave the room and close and lock the door or section off the area to prevent others from entering.

- If you're dealing with a box or package that you suspect contains a bomb, do not put it in a drawer or closet. Leave it on the desk or counter, open any nearby windows to alleviate gases in case of an explosion and lock the door when leaving.

- Wash your hands with soap and cold water, then rewash with warm water.

- Have a spray bottle containing a solution of one-part household bleach and 10 parts water for decontamination use.

- Notify the police.

- Provide authorities with a list of people who were in the room or area when the suspicious item was recognized.

5 CHAPTER FIVE

- Medical Insurance
- Security Travel Tips
- Close Call

...He protected us on our entire journey and among all the nations through which we traveled.

JOSHUA 24:17 (NIV)

MEDICAL INSURANCE

Check with your insurance company to see if coverage applies during travel, both domestic and international. Individuals traveling should also check with their insurance companies to see if coverage exists. Many times, a person's insurance company will contract coverage through a large medical insurance company that handles international travel.

The most significant risk lies in international travel. Usually, medical treatment will be on a cash-only basis in a foreign country. International insurance companies can reimburse costs or arrange for payment for services rendered through third parties located in a foreign country. One such company partners with medical professionals around the world, working with them directly to provide care through 24/7 care centers.

Group rates could cover all people traveling on mission trips. These policies typically renew yearly. Ask if the company covers medical evacuation in the case of serious illness, injury or death. You can pick which services a company offers based on your needs and compare companies through references and other clients.

Here are some of the services that these companies offer:

- Pre-trip medical referral
- 24-hour worldwide medical assistance
- Hourly updates on medical and security concerns around the world on a client-accessed web page
- Emergency medication
- Emergency evacuation
- Continued medical monitoring while hospitalized
- Supervised (escorted) medical repatriation
- Return of human remains (death while traveling)
- Emergency family travel arrangements
- Interpreter services
- Emergency personal cash
- Emergency message transmission
- Lost document assistance
- Deposit guarantee for hospital admission
- Security consultation

SECURITY TRAVEL TIPS

Whether you're traveling to another part of the U.S. or getting ready to go on a church-sponsored mission trip to a foreign country, these tips will help you. Air travel can be cumbersome at times. Expect security checks and occasional long lines. Always show up early to check in to avoid missing your flight.

Pre-Departure Considerations

- Do not place your home address on luggage tags. Use your business address without the organization's name. Do not use a laminated business card as your luggage tag.

- Check to see if your homeowner's insurance policy covers stolen personal effects (such as cameras, laptops, etc.) while traveling.

- Never place valuables in your checked luggage.

- Don't leave bags unattended and keep all bags locked.

- Get your personal affairs in order (power of attorney, will, etc.).

- If you are a frequent flyer, consider getting a TSA pre-check clearance. It currently costs $85 and is valid for five years.

EXAMPLE CLOSE CALL

While on a mission trip to a developing nation, a pastor fell ill and faced medical evacuation to the U.S. The church did not have medical assistance insurance, and the evacuation was estimated to cost $92,000. Fortunately, a three-day stay in a hospital improved the pastor's condition, enabling him to fly home on a commercial flight.

International Travel

- Obtain international health insurance.
- Get information on the country you are visiting from your in-country contact and the following U.S. government websites:
  - CDC.gov/Travel
  - Travel.State.gov
- Place a copy of the photograph and identity pages of your passport in your checked luggage. Carry several copies of your passport and visa photos.
- Avoid unsafe airlines.
- Guard your laptop against theft and get software protection to prevent unauthorized access. Do not leave your backpack containing your laptop and valuables in a car or van, even if the vehicle is locked.
- Leave any credit cards that you are not going to use at home.
- If you plan on driving, check with your local AAA or AATA office to see if you need to obtain an international driver's permit.
- Get a medical checkup. If you take medication, take a double supply on the trip.
- Pack an extra pair of glasses.

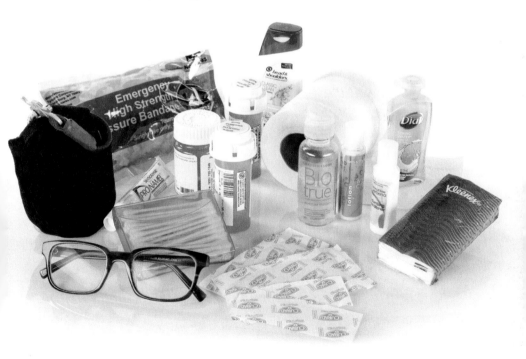

- Obtain information on unique customs and restrictions in the countries you are visiting. In Cuba, for example, it is illegal to take pictures of police stations and military installations.

- You'll want to obtain foreign currency before you leave. International travelers make tempting targets if criminals observe them obtaining large amounts of foreign money from banks and foreign exchange windows at the airport.

- Banks, credit card and travel cheque companies, such as AAA, offer a declining balance credit card. One major benefit to the card is that additional money can be loaded onto the card by someone back home. As with all credit cards used in a foreign country, exchange rates fluctuate frequently.

- Do not send any money or valuables through the mail to a foreign country. Check with your bank and your in-country contact on the process of sending money to the country you are visiting.

- If possible, avoid arriving during hours of darkness.

- Keep your personal space secure. I understand that in large crowds, on trains or streets, this may not be possible. The general rule is not to let anyone help with your luggage that is not a porter or hotel employee. Also, carry a money belt under your clothes. If you find yourself in a crowd, shift your purse or backpack to the front of your body, then place your hand over the zipper or latch. Thieves will open the zipper or cut the bag or backpack next to the zipper, then remove the contents. Trained individuals, including women and children, can do this in a matter of seconds. Be especially aware of ladies carrying small babies that invade your space and linger or start a conversation. They could be using the baby as a distraction.

Warnings

Before going on any trip abroad, check the webpage of the Center for Disease Control at CDC.gov and enter the name of the country you are visiting in the search box, or call 1-800-232-4636. The CDC will provide medical alerts and inoculation recommendations. Check early as some vaccinations require a lead-time of months before a trip.

6 CHAPTER SIX

- Getting Started
- Security Team Selection
- Tragedy Strikes
- Pastor Protection

But we prayed to our God and posted a guard day and night to meet this threat.

NEHEMIAH 4:9 (NIV)

> *"We don't want to have security. It detracts from our welcoming image. I'll put my trust in God, and except for a few highly publicized incidents, crime against churches rarely happen."*

With recent active shooter incidents in houses of worship, fewer church leaders are echoing the above statement. More people are asking for, and in some cases demanding, that their house of worship provide security. It is common to see off-duty, uniformed officers acting as security in most medium to large churches across the country. Even the smallest churches have formed volunteer security teams.

Active shooter events garner the most publicity, but religious leaders have learned that other crimes occur more frequently on their premises. Theft, assault and burglary are common reports. It is difficult to find statistics on crimes committed on church property, as there is no national repository for that data. For instance, a burglary would be listed as a burglary, not as a "church crime" or "church burglary."

GETTING STARTED

Seek a Buy-In

Leadership support is a necessity. A question might be: Will the presence of security be a distraction when people come to church? When done correctly, the answer is "no." Most people expect to see some form of security. They already see security when they attend concerts, basketball games or movies. Your goal is to create a safe place while balancing security and ministry.

Security Committee

Form a committee made up of professionals. They could be active or retired, public or private security professionals. If your congregation's size permits, have a cross section of people from the public and private sectors. Police officers are great when it comes to laws and how to apply them but may not be well-versed in security alarms, security cameras or personal protection. It's always a good idea to have an elder or deacon representing the church on the committee.

Here are a few functions of the group:

- Form a security team
- Meet with local law enforcement
- Create a protocol for the team
- Train staff and volunteers

- Create standards and procedures for protection of the pastor
- Act as a liaison between the church and law enforcement
- Work with church leadership on policy, such as whether to allow concealed weapons on the property
- Investigate and document criminal activity

SECURITY TEAM SELECTION

Whether you are a church of 100 people or 10,000 people, act now to assemble a team. Violence occurs in churches of all sizes. There will be a high level of responsibility given to team members, so vet them carefully. Here are suggestions when putting together your security team.

- **Current Law Enforcement:** Having current law enforcement personnel on the team is a plus. They are officers 24/7 and respond to any call for assistance as an officer. Additionally, most city and county agencies across the country allow officers to work off-duty. Churches hire these officers for traffic duty and security. They are considered contractors and not employees of the church. Large police departments may have a coordinator assigned to handle off-duty officers who can assist with your staffing needs. When hiring an off-duty officer, have him or her work in uniform with a marked police vehicle. A marked unit parked close to the front entrance of your building is an excellent deterrent to criminal activity, and it gives the officer direct communication with his agency in case of an emergency.

    Current officers can also volunteer on your team. While most volunteer officers would rather not be in uniform while attending worship with their families, they can still be a valuable part of your team in the worship center. Inform the officer that while he or she is part of the team, attention should be on duties and not the sermon. Observation and situational awareness are key.

- **Retired Law Enforcement:** A second group to consider is retired law enforcement personnel. These former officers have skills that can help your church. They can obtain a "qualified retired or separated law enforcement officer" concealed carry permit under the federal Law Enforcement Officers Safety Act (LEOSA). This act allows them to carry a concealed firearm in any jurisdiction in the United States regardless of state or local laws, with certain restrictions. They must annually meet the current standards and qualifications in firearms training for active law enforcement officers, as outlined by the law enforcement agency where they reside and register. Their knowledge and current firearms training separate them from most civilians who carry concealed weapons.

- **Military or Former Military:** Whenever I was approached by military or former military personnel looking to join my church's security team, I would ask: "What are you doing (or have done) in the military that would qualify you to be a part of the team?" You are seeking someone proficient and very comfortable with carrying a concealed handgun. Not everyone in the military possesses these traits.

- **Non-Law Enforcement or Non-Military Church Member:** Some churches may not have the luxury of recruiting someone with law enforcement or military experience. In this case, you'll be reaching out to congregational members who you feel can contribute to providing a safe and secure environment. Require designated concealed carry members to undergo firearms training above and beyond a firearms safety class. Consider joining the United States Concealed Carry Association (USCCA) and seek out a certified trainer in your area.

- **Armed vs. Unarmed Security Team:** I'm a firm believer that someone on the team must be armed. Smaller churches may have only two or three members on the team. Each of them should carry a weapon while volunteering. Larger churches may have large teams with everyone on the team carrying a concealed weapon. The concern here is stationing team members in positions that would not cause a problem if an active shooter were to surface in a worship setting. You do not want to injure innocent bystanders with crossfire.

- **Armed vs. Unarmed, Non-Security Team:** Should you allow non-security team members to carry weapons? I've visited churches that do not allow anyone to carry a weapon, including the security team. Other churches allow only the security team to carry and a few churches allow everyone attending to carry. In fact, one church had a sign on the front door notifying the "bad guys" that people are carrying deadly weapons. The leadership of your house of worship must decide who can carry concealed, and in some cases, open carry firearms.

  Note: Your church is considered private property, allowing you to determine who can or cannot carry a weapon on your property. If you decide to prohibit concealed carry on your property, consult with your local law enforcement agency on how to handle someone who refuses to comply with your request. Most agencies will require you to ask the offender to leave the property. If he or she refuses, the offender is subject to a criminal charge for trespassing.

  Some jurisdictions may have laws already in place regarding weapons on church property. For instance, in Georgia, guns are not allowed "in a place of worship, unless the governing body or authority of the place of worship permits the carrying of weapons or long guns by license holders." Anyone violating this law is committing a misdemeanor and will have to pay a fine.

- **Background Checks:** As part of the vetting process, you must run a National Criminal Background Check and a National Sex Offender Registry check on every prospective team member. These checks can be performed by the same company that runs checks for your children's volunteers. Also, as with children's volunteer applicants, ask for three references and do not place the volunteer until you have contacted all three.

Parking Lot Volunteers

Whether your church has 50 parking spaces or 500, every congregation should have someone stationed in the parking lot to welcome people and to help them park their vehicles. This is your front line or first line of security. Outfit the volunteers with a traffic vest, a traffic wand and a church radio. Train them to spot anything unusual and to report it immediately to the security team via two-way radio. In a large church, identify one volunteer to carry a radio while working with other volunteers in a section or parking lot.

Ushers and Greeters

Ushers and greeters form your second line of security. Position them in the church to greet everyone as they enter the building. Longtime members who recognize many of the church's members and are good at spotting a first-time visitor make excellent greeters. Training is vital for this group. Here are some points that can be passed on to the ushers and greeters:

- Maintain a friendly and welcoming attitude.

- Look for visitors.

- Introduce yourself and ask the visitor his/her name. In a smaller church, this will occur at the front door. In a larger church, a section host in the worship center will do this. Remember, the bad guys do not want to be identified.

- Have the greeter look for any suspicious behavior, such as someone trying to avoid them, wearing heavy or bulky clothing in hot weather, appearing nervous or excessively sweating.

- Remind ushers to inform security immediately if someone makes them feel uncomfortable. They should not wait!

- Ushers should walk through the worship center before, between and after every service. Look for items that the security team needs to investigate, like an unattended box or backpack. Watch for people that seem out of place. They may be in prayer or contemplation, but if they make you feel uncomfortable, notify security.

Traffic Control/Security

People coming to services usually arrive close together. For their safety and the safety of others in traffic, you may have to provide traffic control. This control may be as simple as having volunteers directing traffic in your parking lots or as sophisticated as hiring off-duty uniformed officers to direct traffic. These officers can direct traffic by controlling traffic lights or standing in the roadway. Once traffic is "in," the uniformed officer(s) can be brought in and around your building to provide security. The following are general traffic rules:

- Use law enforcement officers on public roadways. You'll increase the church's liability, in case of an accident, if you are using civilians to direct traffic on a public road.
- Use officers to control traffic lights.
- Use trained volunteers on church property.
- Post someone at each crosswalk to help pedestrians.
- Equip traffic officers with church radios.

Be sensitive to traffic that is passing through. Do not hold the line up too long. Be a good neighbor. I've found that the threshold for stopped traffic is between three and four minutes.

EXAMPLE TRAGEDY STRIKES

In 2003, a woman shot and killed her pastor, her mother and then herself in an Atlanta church on a Sunday morning. Witnesses reported that the suspect and her mother were arranging the communion table when the pastor greeted them. She then pulled out a handgun and shot him. As people ran from the church, she shot and killed her mother, then herself.

PASTOR PROTECTION

With crime on the rise, we must be ever vigilant with protecting our assets. The greatest of these is our people. Adopt a proactive stance to deter criminal activity rather than responding after a crime is committed. Personal protection also helps dispel any false accusations of personal misconduct (integrity issues) that someone could levy against your leaders. With this in mind, take a hard look at protecting your KEY individuals. The security committee, with consultation from your leadership team, will determine the scope of this protection. In smaller churches, the senior pastor should have protection. In larger churches, protection would extend to his associates. If there is a perceived level of threat, protection may extend to families or other staff members.

Who protects the pastor? Your first choice should be a plainclothes volunteer police officer from your team. Use another team member if you do not have an officer available. If a confrontation or incident occurs and the assailant is injured, who will be held liable in a criminal or civil complaint? If the volunteer is a sworn law enforcement officer, his or her actions are usually covered by the agency as the officer is acting under protection provided by local or state law. If he or she is not currently a sworn officer, then the church may be held liable.

Making a Plan

Discuss the following guidelines when formulating a plan:

- Talk to the ministers to determine their needs. Explain your requirements and come up with a workable solution.

- Twenty-four-hour protection is usually not needed unless a threat exists.

- The pastor's home should have a security system.

- The pastor and his family must always carry cellphones.

- During weekend services, consider meeting the pastor when he parks his vehicle and stay with him until he leaves.

- My recommendation is to not schedule counseling during the weekend.

- Keep protection during services low-key and professional. The distance between security and the person you are protecting will be determined by what he or she is doing. Walking in a hallway may dictate walking alongside. When he or she stops to talk to someone, it may be wise to step a few feet away. You are in a church setting, so act accordingly.

- **Train, train, train!** Get professional training, even if you must pay for it. A federal or local law enforcement officer trained in personal/executive protection can provide this training. You'll find most mid- to large-sized police agencies include staff trained in executive protection. Brief the trainer on your expectations as you try to balance protection within a church setting.

- If possible, do not allow someone to protect your pastor or minister unless he or she has gone through protective training.

- Keep the personal protection group small. This intimacy will help the protectee feel comfortable with the team.

- Have a "safe room" close to the podium or stage. This room could also serve as a music room or even a storage room, but it must have a deadbolt in a solid and heavier-than-normal door. If you are designing this room or retrofitting it, install a solid ceiling and reinforce the walls, especially around the door. The pastor will be taken to this room if something happens while speaking at the podium. Many times, the disrupter's anger or statements will be directed at the pastor and removing him will deflate the situation into a manageable event. One person should remove the pastor while others on the security team handle the situation. Do not exit the building unless you must.

- Put someone in charge. During non-emergency times, usually the person with the pastor is the person in charge; however, this is only a general rule of thumb. If an emergency occurs and you are using law enforcement officers, then the highest-ranking officer would immediately take command.

Pastoral Counseling

Part of your overall security plan should include protecting the integrity of your pastor. Pastoral counseling can cause concerns in this area. Unless the pastor is counseling a friend, I recommend that he does not do any personal counseling around weekend services. If he chooses to do counseling, do not allow him to engage in private sessions with a female. Schedule counseling during regular daytime office hours. After two sessions, the pastor should refer the person or couple to a professional counselor.

7 CHAPTER SEVEN

THE ACTIVE SHOOTER

May the Lord answer you when you are in distress; may the name of the God of Jacob protect you.

PSALM 20:1

> *"An active shooter is an individual actively engaged in killing or attempting to kill people in a confined and populated area; in most cases, active shooters use firearms and there is no pattern or method to their selection of victims."*
>
> U.S. Department of Homeland Security

STATISTICS

Getting accurate statistics on crime in houses of worship, specifically active shooters, is difficult. As I mentioned earlier in the book, there is no national repository for church crime. A few organizations attempt to track active shooter incidents, but they employ disparate standards. Some include church shootings and crime in and around the church, while others focus on all violent crimes in and around the church.

The FBI has tracked all active shooter events. Here are the statistics for 2016 and 2017:

- There were 20 active shooter events in 2016 and 39 events in 2017.

- In 2017, 138 people were killed and 593 wounded. This was the highest count since 2000.

- All shooters in 2016 and 2017 were men.

- Thirteen of the gunmen committed suicide. Police killed 11 and civilians killed eight. Police took the others into custody.

- Most incidents were over within five to 10 minutes.

Although shootings happen infrequently in houses of worship, the events can be devastating — not only to the families and the congregation directly affected but also to other places of worship across the country. Everyone wonders if it could happen to them and if they have adequately prepared. Size doesn't matter, as evidenced by the Sutherland Springs, Texas, shooting. Your resources may be limited, but with guidance and training, you can provide a more secure environment for your members and visitors.

August 1999
North Valley Jewish Community Center, Granada Hills, California

A white supremacist shot and killed one person and wounded five others. The killer had a map outlining three other Jewish centers but drove by when he saw uniformed security at all three locations. Three days later, he walked into the lobby of North Valley and opened fire with a submachine gun. The shooter wounded a receptionist, camp counselor and three boys. He fled the scene in his vehicle. A few minutes later, he carjacked a woman's car and left his vehicle at a nearby motel. The assailant later approached a USPS employee delivering mail a few miles from North Valley and asked him a question. During the conversation, the man shot and killed the postal employee. He then took a taxi to Las Vegas and ultimately gave himself up by walking into an FBI office.

September 1999
Wedgewood Baptist Church, Ft. Worth, Texas

A dangerous man walked into the church during a concert for high school students. The show was part of a night of worship and prayer. The terrorist walked in the central rear doors, shot an adult male sitting in the back pew, rolled a pipe bomb under the benches and began shooting as people hid under seats. The pipe bomb detonated, but everyone escaped injury. However, the man killed eight people and wounded seven others before turning the gun on himself.

SOFT TARGET / HARD TARGET

For our purposes, soft targets are "a house of worship that is unprotected or vulnerable to attack." Hard targets are "houses of worship that have taken protective measures to minimize risks." The presence of a uniformed officer or a marked police vehicle denote a hardened target. Given a choice, shooters will choose soft targets over hard targets.

CAUSES

Every shooting situation varies. After every event, security professionals want to know why it happened — to learn how they can prepare, prevent, respond and recover. The following is a list of categories into which I believe most active shooters (who target houses of worship) fall:

- **A Difference of Religious Opinion/Ideology:** He may not agree with the church's stance on a social topic, such as abortion or same-sex marriage. He may not agree with the church's partnerships with other churches who do not share the same denomination or ethnicity. He might hate Jews, Muslims, Christians or other faith groups.

- **Domestic Disputes:** Family disputes can escalate into violence. All churches have dealt with divorce, custody battles, family arguments, etc. Some people do not like confrontation, so instead of talking it out, they'll "solve" the problem by killing the person with whom they have a difference. Your members need to know that they can talk to someone in authority at your church about what they perceive as a possible threat. Your staff and volunteers in children and youth ministry should communicate with church authorities regarding any family issues they overhear.

- **Youth Issues:** Staff and volunteers should pay attention to youth who display signs of threatening language, outbursts of anger, antisocial or strange behavior and bullying. Seek help immediately for the child and monitor his or her behavior and that of nearby children.

- **Retribution:** The church may have told the person that he can no longer be a member. His wife or children may have been embarrassed by a statement someone made while attending church. The children's ministry may have disciplined his child. There could be several reasons, and churches deal with these regularly. Communicate openly to the person involved. You want this to end well. Some people hold grudges for a long time and will return to right the wrong.

- **Mental Illness:** Mental illness can manifest itself in many forms, including depression, bipolar disorder, anxiety, violence and schizophrenia. I've experienced congregational members who stop taking required medication because they feel great. When this happens, you will need to deal with the situation. It is crucial to learn who these people are and to recognize the behavior. Solicit help from a family member or friend of the person. Don't wait. I'll also place in this category the shooter who wants to become famous. He has serious psychological issues. He envisions his picture and story being shown over and over on the news, as the national media are prone to do. It is for this reason that no mass shooters have been mentioned by name in this book.

- **Workplace Violence:** Meet with your human resources person or department head to determine how your staff reports any troubling behavior they recognize in other staff members. Train your staff on what to look for and whom to call. The threat may come from someone's spouse or partner who is involved in a domestic dispute with them. Your staff should not hesitate to inform you of this, as it could escalate to a violent outcome. Be especially vigilant in disciplinary and termination meetings.

PREPARATION

- Invite police, fire and EMS to visit your facility. Have them look at it as if they were responding to an active shooter. Ask for recommendations and put them in place. Take these to heart, as they may be life-saving tips. If you're in a city large enough to have an FBI office, ask them out as well. Create a contact list of representatives from each of these agencies. I've partnered with a metro police department that hosted an active shooter training session for houses of worship. Representatives from more than 200 churches attended. This opened lines of communication between the police department and the houses of worship.

- SWAT teams and K-9 units are always looking for new places to train. Of course, the training takes place when the building is not in use. It will give you a chance to meet the teams, and the units will become familiar with your facility. This familiarity will help tremendously in case of an emergency.

- The United States Concealed Carry Association (USCCA) has filmed a set of active shooter training videos for houses of worship. The scenario-based videos are part of the *Proving Ground* series. Lessons learned can be applied to churches of any size. I believe they are the best training videos out there and represent a must-see for all security personnel involved in protecting houses of worship. Call 844-291-9224 or visit the USCCA website at USConcealedCarry.com.

EXAMPLE
CHURCH ACTIVE SHOOTER INCIDENTS

December 2007
New Life Christian Church, Colorado Springs, Colorado

A man shot and killed two teenage sisters as they exited their family's car in the church parking lot. He also wounded their father and another adult female as she tried to get into her vehicle. He attempted to shoot others but missed and hit only vehicles. The attacker then entered the church through the main entrance and wounded an adult male who had tried to distract him by yelling. A female volunteer security officer confronted the shooter as he turned down a hallway where teenagers were running out of the building. The volunteer, a former police officer, exchanged gunfire with the invader, who died of a head wound. The final report did not say if the assailant died of a self-inflicted gunshot wound or if the volunteer fired the fatal shot.

At around 12:30 a.m., the day of the shooting, the gunman had visited the training center of Youth With a Mission in nearby Arvada. He was a one-time resident of the home but was asked to leave the program before completing training. After knocking on the door, the deranged man asked two staff members if he could stay the night. During the conversation, he shot and killed both staff members and injured two others. He fled the scene and resurfaced at New Life Christian Church that afternoon, killing the two teenagers and wounding three others.

TRAINING

- **Security Team:** Seek out experts to train your team. Check with your local police agency, your insurance company and organizations such as the USCCA and the American Society for Industrial Security (ASIS) for recommendations. Your team has many responsibilities, but let me touch on a few considerations. Use plain language when conversing on radios. Ten codes can be confusing when you have personnel from different agencies and non-law enforcement working together.

  In a smaller house of worship, placing team members in your worship center can be as easy as putting one person in the rear and one up front, on each side of the stage. This allows them a clear view of most of the seating. In larger worship centers, the team would have one on each side up front, one in the back, one in the lobby and one in the balcony. All unlocked doors into the building should have someone on the inside with a radio, even if it's a non-team member. At a minimum, someone should walk through the children and youth areas. At best, assign someone to each area.

- **Staff and Volunteers:** Establish mandatory active shooter training for all staff and weekend volunteers. Give a brief overview of how the security team will respond and what the duties entail. Teach them the location of emergency exits. Depending on where they are, tell them always to have a first and second choice, in case something or someone is blocking the primary exit.

  Talk about the A.L.I.C.E. and "Run, Hide, Fight" methods of responding to an active shooter. Certified trainers teach the A.L.I.C.E. method, and many school districts have embraced it. It's also gaining

EXAMPLE
CHURCH ACTIVE SHOOTER INCIDENTS

August 2012
Gurdwara Sikh Temple, Oak Creek, Wisconsin

A lone gunman shot and killed three people outside and three people inside the temple. Two others were wounded. The first police officer on the scene, Lt. Brian Murphy, was shot 15 times by the assailant. Miraculously, Murphy survived. After being shot by another police officer, the perpetrator killed himself. Reports indicated that the murderer had ties to white supremacist groups.

traction in small businesses. Safety and security professionals across the country teach the widespread "Run, Hide, Fight" method. No certification is needed to teach it. You'll want to teach only one method to avoid confusion.

The Department of Homeland Security partnered with the Houston Police Department to produce an excellent six-minute video, available on YouTube, titled "RUN, HIDE, FIGHT. Surviving an Active Shooter Event." The video is set in an office environment and demonstrates what to do if an active shooting takes place in your building. You can easily apply the video's lessons to any environment. The information is incredibly useful. I believe that every adult and teenager you know should watch it.

- **Ushers and Greeters:** Meet with this group at least quarterly to talk about security. This keeps the awareness level up and gives the group meembers an opportunity to ask questions or share what they've seen or done in the last three months regarding security incidents or concerns. Ushers and greeters should be well-versed in emergency routes out of the building. If the shooter is not close by, the ushers could help people escape. Think of assigning a door to each usher or greeter in case of evacuation. In large churches, assign an usher to a seating section and assign a specific door to which he should direct the flow of evacuees. Post a map of the worship center with evacuation routes and section assignments in the usher room.

- **Children and Youth:** Lead staff members or volunteers in each area must carry radios capable of contacting security. Someone needs to be free to walk the hallways or classroom areas during services, looking for anything unusual. Many churches lock down the children's area once service starts to prevent any unauthorized entry. Your lead staff member or volunteer in the hallway can admit late arrivals. Each classroom must have doors that teachers or students can lock from the inside. Instruct teachers on how to lock down and shelter in place. Companies sell specialized equipment for securing doors, such as metal barricades. These may violate fire codes so check with your Fire Marshal before you make a purchase.

- **Parking Lot Volunteers:** Don't forget these volunteers. Meet with them quarterly. Remind them that awareness and observation will usually allow them to see something before the security team does. They are your first level of security with the ability to spot a potential perpetrator and communicate to security his location, description, path or direction, etc.

- **Cellphones:** I've seen incredible advances in technology in my lifetime. One of the most amazing of which is the cellphone. When I left the house as a kid, my mom would give me a dime to make a call from a pay phone in case of an emergency. Today it seems everyone has a cellphone. My 3-year-old grandson has already been offered a cellphone from a relative. Thankfully, my daughter said no.

  I visited a church that hired off-duty uniformed police officers to control traffic and security. When my wife and I walked in a few minutes before the service, four off-duty uniformed officers were standing at the four exterior doors into the main atrium. All of them had their heads down looking at their cellphones. I could have easily walked by them openly carrying a weapon, and they would not have stopped me. Your team and the men and women you hire are there to provide a safe place for your congregation. PUT THE CELLPHONES AWAY!

- **Gunshot Detection Systems:** It's important to confirm that gunfire has occurred and where it's happening. Throughout the country, outdoor gunshot detection systems assist local law enforcement in recognizing and quickly responding to possible violent crime. I know of a large manufacturing facility that has installed detectors in key areas of the plant. Notification is done through emergency texts, flashing lights or audible devices broadcasting instructions. Integrate one or all of these into the system along with the ability to automatically alert local authorities. I took part in a demonstration of the system in an office building. It did what it was advertised to do. If you are part of large or megachurch, I recommend you look into a gunshot detection system.

November 2017
First Baptist Church, Sutherland Springs, Texas

At about 11:20 a.m. during a church service, a man exited his vehicle and started shooting. He was wearing a bullet-resistant vest and tactical gear. He killed two people before taking his shooting spree into the church. Once inside, he shot and killed 24 people and wounded 20 more. Authorities believe that a domestic dispute with his mother-in-law predicated the shooting. An FBI investigator estimated the man had fired more than 400 rounds during the rampage. One report indicated investigators found 15 empty magazines, each with a capacity of 30 rounds. At the time of the shooting, a neighbor was getting ready for work when his daughter told him she heard gunshots coming from the First Baptist Church. A former NRA instructor and competitive shooter, the civilian grabbed his firearm and ran outside toward the church. As the assailant exited the church, he saw the neighbor and started shooting. The neighbor returned fire, but the attacker made it to his vehicle and drove away, firing his weapon. The good Samaritan noticed a passer-by sitting in his pickup at a stop sign, got in and told him to chase the fleeing car. The assailant killed himself after wrecking his vehicle.

October 2018
Kroger Marketplace, Jeffersontown, Kentucky

An armed man walked into Kroger and shot and killed an African American male in a shopping aisle. He then walked out and shot and killed an African American female in the parking lot. As the shooter approached his vehicle, an armed civilian exchanged gunfire with him. Neither the shooter nor the civilian were injured. As the attacker was pulling away, police officers arrived. He was stopped and arrested. About 15 minutes before the shooting at Kroger, the shooter had attempted to enter a predominantly African American church nearby. Surveillance video caught him banging on and pulling the front door, which was locked. A small group of staff and congregational members were in the church. A staff member said, "If he would have come by about 30 minutes earlier, 70 people were in church with the doors unlocked."

RESPONSE

Active shooters are unpredictable, and most active shooter events are over in a few minutes. Is the shooter targeting an individual or group? Is this a random act of violence? You may not know what type of gun he's using, but it doesn't matter. You've prepared and trained; now it's time to act.

- **Congregation:** People often ask how I think the congregation will react when a shooter stands and starts firing. I was fortunate to be a part of the USCCA's scenario-based active shooter training videos in which we used church members, friends and business associates to play the part of a congregation. Producers informed them that they would be in an active-shooter scenario (with no live-fire weapons involved), but they offered no training or advice on what to do when the actor started shooting. The actor playing the role of the shooter integrated with the crowd as if he were part of the congregation.

  When he started firing, people dove behind chairs, mothers covered their children, others ran for exits and one man "played dead." One individual, who apparently had gone through some training, yelled "RUN, RUN, RUN!" as he ran for an exit. We held an after-action discussion and training session with the congregation, then ran the scenario a second time. The difference was that more people ran for the doors. However, one constant remained: For the first few seconds, almost everyone ducked or crouched behind chairs — even those who eventually ran.

- **Ushers:** If you're at a door, run out of the building to a safe area. Take as many people with you as you safely can, but don't stay. People may be in disbelief or shock, so if you must, yell at them to get out as you are leaving. Call 911 when you get out. Don't assume that someone else is doing it.

- **Security:** You're in your security position in the worship center when the shooting starts. I stated earlier that the congregation took cover for a few seconds before some of them ran. This is your chance to get up, acquire your target and close the gap between you and him as quickly as possible. This must be done in one fluid trained movement, as you have only a few seconds to stop the violence.

EXAMPLE
CHURCH ACTIVE SHOOTER INCIDENTS

October 2018
Tree of Life Synagogue, Pittsburgh, Pennsylvania

A deranged killer, armed with multiple firearms, drove to the Tree of Life Synagogue where three congregations were conducting services. He shot a window next to the main doors, then entered the building. He shot two men inside the front entrance and headed downstairs to one of the services. There, he shot four people then climbed the stairs to another group meeting. He killed seven more and wounded one while five escaped. A total of 11 people lost their lives and two others suffered injuries during the shooting. When police arrived a few minutes later, the murderer opened fire from the building's entryway. Police returned fire, and he retreated into the building. SWAT teams entered the building and located the man on the third floor. An exchange of gunfire wounded the terrorist and two officers. The man surrendered and told officers he wanted all Jews to die. Authorities levied a 63-count indictment against him, 13 of which describe violations of the Federal Hate Crimes Prevention Act. About 15 days before the shooting, the man had posted statements on a website condemning Jewish congregations, including one of the groups meeting at Tree of Life.

Police Response

In our first training video, the security team member (a police officer) had received no training on how to respond to a shooter in a house of worship. When the shooter stood and started firing, the officer created distance, took cover and started shooting. However, he had created too much distance between himself and the shooter. In the second scenario, we instructed the officer to close the gap and take the shooter out. We did not tell the shooter what we had said to the officer. When the officer closed the distance and started shooting, it caught the shooter by surprise and allowed the officer to fire his weapon at close range. The officer neutralized the shooter.

Practice this as a team to avoid crossfire and hitting innocent people. Run different training scenarios for your team. What if the shooter enters elsewhere in the building, such as the children's area, gym or youth center? If you utilize off-duty officers, include them in your training.

- **What to do when officers arrive:** It's imperative that your team and your congregation understand what to do — and what not to do — when help comes. Law enforcement will want to stop the threat and secure the scene. You don't want to increase the danger for innocent bystanders during this timeframe. Thus, some things to consider and train for include:

  - Do not run toward the officers.
  - Remain calm. Do not scream or yell.
  - Follow instructions. Be cooperative and answer questions.
  - Show them your hands.
  - Do not stop them to ask for help. Their job is to find the shooter.

Recovery

The shooter is down and the violence has stopped. Now what? If law enforcement is on the scene, they take the lead and you assist as needed. If not, you must act with authority while waiting for the authorities. Here are some actions to take:

- Have someone on the phone with the authorities providing information so they can determine what resources are needed.
- Attend to the injured and ask for medical assistance.
- Secure the scene. Do not let any civilians into the scene unless they are needed.

- Provide counseling for anyone on site and the families of victims. If needed, ask for help from other houses of worship.
- Notify your minister, church leadership and insurance company.
- Appoint a liaison to work with law enforcement and media.
- Assign a team member or trusted volunteer to create an event timeline, including post-event activity.

Lastly, the scene will be chaotic and people will likely be in various stages of shock. You have just been through a traumatic event. Take a deep breath, remain calm and take charge. My son has a saying at his place of employment, "Do whatever it takes." In other words, take time to make sure everyone is taken care of and everything will fall into place.

DEFENDING HOUSES OF WORSHIP
What to Do Before Your Church Becomes a Target

By George Harris

A ll of us who celebrate the Sabbath in our chosen religions, whether it be during the weekly services or in group meetings held at different times, need to be aware of the potential threats to our safety — much as in any other gathering of people. Many of us think of our religions as "peace-loving" and that our places of worship are safe from any conflict or violence. You have but to read the scriptures or the history books to see that there has always been disagreement leading to physical aggression, up to and including all-out war, between — and often within — religious sects. Just because it hasn't yet happened in your locale, doesn't mean it isn't happening regularly in other parts of the country or the world.

Sadly, unless there is a high body count or some other distinguishing factor to sell advertising, the media won't cover it on a wide scale.

For those of you thinking that this is a recent phenomenon, I'd like to relate a personal experience. My dad was a Methodist minister whose job was to go as a missionary into the mountainous areas of southwestern Virginia. He was sent there to organize a congregation and to establish and build a church. He would then pass off the working and thriving religious group to another minister before moving to his next assignment.

In one of my dad's appointed areas, the production of "moonshine whiskey" employed many of the locals. As my dad went about his work building his "flock," one of the more prominent local bootleggers noted that production and profits were taking a downturn due to my dad's efforts. One Sunday, while my dad was holding services, the bootlegger entered the church and fired a shot into the ceiling. He proclaimed that he was going to kill the S.O.B. that was ruining his business. My dad and the rest of the occupants bailed out of any available opening and left the building to the bootlegger. The story got a happy ending when a local sheriff, who happened to be a relative of the bootlegger, mediated a peaceful solution between the two differing parties. The local inhabitants were allowed to make their own choice as to which road they wanted to follow.

I do know that my dad, who had never owned a gun, traded a banjo to his brother for a S&W .38 Special just in case an incident like that happened again. Fortunately, it never did.

In researching this article, I decided to paint this subject with a pretty broad brush to stimulate thought and perhaps provide a few answers. Out of respect for the churches of various religions — those that agreed to discuss their plans and preparations for an active shooter event — all will remain anonymous in the interest of safety.

I contacted a church with 35 active members, places of worship with thousands of members and memberships that fell between the two. I polled congregation members from the corners to the middle of the country — as well as a few outside of the country — as to how they and their fellow members would respond to an active shooter during a religious gathering. Individual trainers and security groups that were involved with church security — as well as organized police, EMS and other potential responders — were asked for input into this very real and interesting subject.

Realizing that there could be legal implications that would influence the thinking of the congregation and church leadership, I consulted several attorneys.

I also took a Protective Shooting Class from Scott Ballard at the SIG Sauer Academy (SigSauerAcademy.com) to fully orient my thinking to that of an ordinary citizen who carries a concealed firearm on a daily basis. Some reading this likely have served as cops, military personnel or armed professionals at some point in their lives. These professionals were trained to take charge, control the situation and save the day when trouble presents itself. The day they leave the job for the last time and become civilians again, that mindset often doesn't change. This can prove detrimental in many ways, simply because the game plan has changed.

As a civilian, taking responsibility for the safety of others becomes a personal choice with associated consequences and perspectives. That point was driven home by what Ballard called "the list." "The list" was defined as those whom you would die for, whom you would go to jail for, and whom you would lose all of your possessions and net worth for in order to protect their safety. When put in that perspective, most of our lists aren't too long.

This consideration, added to SIG's reality-based training drills — involving as many as 20 people in close quarters, all having to make decisions one after the other in a perpetually changing hostile environment — showed me that many talk a good game. But when it comes down to performing under pressure, they aren't as good as they think they are. Such training is invaluable for armed confrontations in a house of worship, where the situation is ever-evolving and split-second decisions mean the difference between success and failure.

The two-day class stimulated me to contact friend, attorney, author and guest SIG Sauer Academy Instructor, Andrew Branca, about the legal aspects of personal defense in a house of worship. Branca is the author of the comprehensive book *The Law of Self Defense* (LawOfSelfDefense.com). Discussing this subject at length with Branca and referencing a copy of his newest book validated my thinking that a shooting scenario in a house of worship involves infinite variables. There is no legal immunity for religious activities, meaning that those who carry concealed must also be aware of and abide by the legal restrictions specific to that locale.

Fortunately, most of us attend services at the same location every time. We are familiar with the layout of the building and what layers of security exist in our particular house of worship. If carrying concealed is condoned in your place of worship, it is likely that those who do carry will become acquainted with one another, which helps when things go wrong. The more you plan and organize a course of action, the higher the likelihood that you can prevent or control an active shooter event.

A publication from FEMA (Fema.gov), "Guide to Developing High-Quality Emergency Operations Plans for Houses of Worship," provides some valuable guidelines for dealing with a variety of emergencies likely to affect a place of worship. The publication devotes sections to planning and preparation, prevention and responding to and dealing with the aftermath of an active shooter event. The comprehensive guide provides a useful framework with which to work, although some might find it not as firearm-friendly as they would like. Those who are intent on taking a proactive stance against the potential of an active shooter in their place of worship should read the enlightening report, along with its references.

While researching this article, I found some interesting trends in the preparedness of various religions and houses of worship. Geographically, gun-friendly regions seem to possess a more proactive approach to having an armed, organized congregation. In more politically liberal areas, many worship centers don't feel the need to address the issue. The leadership isn't concerned because it hasn't happened there and presents no recognized threat. The general thinking is that guns aren't welcome, regardless of who carries them. Period!

Exceptions to these liberal attitudes are held by those outside of the predominant religious groups. These smaller groups have been historically looked down upon and persecuted. Some face discrimination and harassment to this very day.

I was amazed by some of the sophisticated safety measures I encountered. Economics, in many cases, dictated the levels of external and internal security. Some of the larger, more affluent groups had hired security professionals to ensure congregational safety. Others chose to keep their security efforts in-house, preferring to be trained by the security professionals but formulating and executing their plans to the exclusion of anyone outside of the group.

The use of trained, organized and armed security seemed to be more prevalent in highly populated areas. The more rural congregations, mainly those smaller in size, relied on a few members who were prepared to defend the rest should an active shooter incident occur.

Many of those with whom I communicated weren't as concerned about an outside attack as they were about an attack from within. They felt that the perimeter of the property and the entrances to the worship hall were relatively easy to control. However, without TSA-type airport screening, there was no way to be sure of what kind of armament was in the worship hall at any given time.

This, of course, adds to the horror of an active shooter incident from within the congregation. With an unknown number of guns present, it would be all but impossible to distinguish the good guys from the bad guys. This, combined with gunfire originating from within a panicked crowd, would inevitably result in unintended collateral damage.

As a hedge to mitigate shooting the wrong individuals, some have organized their known firearms carriers. The responders are to wear brightly colored designators around their necks when a firearms incident takes place. There are other ideas, I'm sure, but the fact remains that if there is a shooting incident in a crowd of people, innocent people are going to get hurt.

The best thing you can do to avoid injury and loss of life is to prevent the attack in the first place. If the signs are there, don't ignore the obvious. Often, we dismiss some cue or clue as unimportant, that, had we acted upon it, could have prevented or attenuated the violence.

Individually, we can be proactive in saving ourselves and the ones on "the list" that I mentioned earlier. Start with simple awareness of the potentials and likelihoods of an active shooter event in your house of worship. Formulate and practice several plans of action to prevent having to come up with one as the event unfolds. As an example, unless you and the shooter are in very close proximity to one another, the best course of action might be to escape. Part of that plan could be where you choose to sit in the meeting hall. Where are the most direct escape routes for you and those on the list? Being too close to an exit might put you in the direct line of fire should the attacker choose that exit as his point of entry. What are your observation capabilities when the congregation is seated and standing? An attack might play out very differently if the group is focused on prayer or joined in song.

Each given situation and place of worship offers unique challenges to ponder. Imagine possible scenarios and have your response to each firmly in mind. Consider your legal parameters, moral values, personal values and obligations in forming your actions. Think of the worst-case scenario and how you would respond to that situation. Think of those on "the list" and how they would fare without you to depend on in the future. These are hard questions for which there are no universal answers.

PREDATORS & PRAY
What Can We Do About Church Shootings?

By David Burnett

On June 17, 2015, one criminal's lone-wolf attack on a prayer service in South Carolina became the latest mass shooting to attract headlines — and fundraising pleas from gun control advocates.

Although authorities found disturbing journals detailing how alone the suspect felt in his prejudice, liberal politicos hailed the attacks as emblematic of systemic racism and used them as a springboard to demand tighter restrictions on the guns in your home. Almost automatically, politicians began musing that new laws could stop future violence. Of course, since South Carolina churches are gun-free zones by law (pending clergy exemption) and since the suspect was not legally permitted to purchase, own or carry a gun, it requires powerful imagination to suppose additional laws would have deterred him.

Every mass shooting sparks discussions of what went wrong and how to further secure target locations — in this case, churches. Spree killings can (and do) happen anywhere, but records indicate church shootings are on the rise.

In May 2015, a Connecticut pastor was wounded in a drive-by shooting while setting up Memorial Day flags outside his Nazarene church. In 2008, a Maryville, Illinois, pastor was gunned down in the middle of his sermon, with witnesses reporting the man unsuccessfully tried to use his Bible as a shield from the gunfire. In 2012, a Wisconsin Sikh temple fell under siege from a lone gunman, who killed six and wounded four. Two Catholic priests were shot in a Phoenix parish in 2014. A 2008 Universalist church shooting left two dead and seven wounded, while a 2007 Missouri church shooting left a pastor and two deacons dead. In 2006, gunfire interrupted a Louisiana service when a gunman shot five people, four fatally, before abducting and murdering his wife.

In February 2016, officials announced the arrest of an Islamic State sympathizer in Dearborn, Michigan, who had intended to commit mass murder at an unidentified Detroit megachurch.

"It's easy, and a lot of people go there," the complaint quotes the would-be assailant. "Plus people are not allowed to carry guns in church."

The circumstances surrounding each of these episodes were different, but the lessons are the same: Murderers have no respect for the church, and it takes more than a Bible to stop a bullet.

Mass murders always leave difficult questions in their wake, but gun owners shouldn't try to avoid those questions. Although ensuing discussions inevitably assume a political bent, it's our humanity — not politics — that obligates us to reject further obstruction of lawfully armed resistance. After all, history is indisputable on two points: Rapid mass murders occur almost exclusively in gun-free zones and increasing access to lawful self-defense can increase the odds of surviving them.

On an individual level, houses of worship are still grappling with how to respond. Large churches often hire security firms or off-duty police officers. Some recruit volunteers, and many have raised awareness — and eyebrows — by hosting concealed carry classes for members. Certain gun shops have offered discounts and classes specifically for clergy. One Louisiana firm, after the Charleston shootings, hosted a class exclusively for area ministers and their spouses. Some ministers go on to carry from the pulpit or incorporate self-defense into their messages.

"We're not in Mayberry anymore," one Catholic priest said in a lengthy statement to his Ann Arbor, Michigan, parish regarding organized concealed carry classes. (Unfortunately, the Diocese bishop superseded the priest and forced the class to cancel.)

One Kentucky church went so far as to host a "Bring Your Gun to Church" day in 2009, and a Dallas-area megachurch invites congregants to carry openly. Others host gun "buy-backs" or candlelight vigils to encourage non-violence.

Bottom line: The church is in on the debate, whether they like it or not.

The federal government recognizes the problem and has issued a "Guide to Developing High-Quality Emergency Operations Plans for Houses of Worship." Although the report noted that potential victims ended 16 of 41 active shooter incidents studied before police arrived, officials only advise fighting back if flight or hiding is not possible. (They suggest using such weapons as "fire extinguishers or chairs.")

In July 2015, the U.S. Attorney's Office hosted a summit in Detroit with officials from the FBI, the Department of Justice and the Department of Homeland Security to discuss threat reduction, action plans and the protection of congregations. Officials recommend holding drills, analyzing and preventing potential threats and planning evacuation routes. In February 2016, the FBI hosted more than 160 faith leaders in Dallas to address the unique dangers faced by houses of worship.

Concealed carry isn't automatically an option. Certain states prohibit worshipping while armed, and even some shooting enthusiasts hesitate to carry in church, uncertain of conflicts with doctrinal orthodoxy. Many civilized congregants are incredulous that anyone would ever need a gun in church.

Retired-lieutenant-turned-minister Lawrence Adams knows better. He routinely wears a concealed pistol beneath his robes. In 2009, he was confronted and attacked by an intruder while responding to an alarm in his Detroit church. Drawing on his police training, Adams pulled a concealed firearm and opened fire.

In July 2015, an armed church employee in Boulder, Colorado, intervened when a drunken man attacked his estranged wife in a church parking lot. As the man stabbed the woman and began strangling her, the employee displayed a firearm and sent the man running. Local sheriff Joe Pelle told reporters that many churchgoers had started carrying in response to church threats.

Also in July 2015, a would-be robber in Baytown, Texas, kicked down a church door, not expecting to find the well-armed pastor Benny Holmes inside. Fearing for his life, Holmes shot the intruder. (Less than a year earlier, Pastor Holmes had apprehended a serial thief at gunpoint in his home.)

Stories such as these provide a cold reality check on the fearful whispers of gun control advocates who claim guns "only make things worse." Indeed, guns aren't the solution to every problem, but they are a solution to some issues, and that includes rapid mass murders.

Charleston's high body count in 2015 dominated headlines, but 200 miles and three years away, another church avoided a similar situation thanks to concealed carry. In March 2012, a felon entered a small Baptist church in South Carolina and pointed a loaded shotgun at the congregation. Parishioner Aaron Guyton drew his concealed handgun and held the intruder at gunpoint, working with the pastor and others to disarm and subdue him. No shots were fired, and authorities praised Guyton for his actions.

"I hope the bad guys are watching because we are tired of your nonsense," Sheriff Chuck Wright told reporters. "People are simply protecting their families. Prepare yourselves, ladies and gentlemen."

Aurora, Colorado, is infamous for its theater murders, but 20 miles and two months away, a felon crashed into an Aurora church parking lot and opened fire on the crowd, killing one. The man was promptly shot dead by the victim's nephew, an off-duty police officer.

Then there's the New Life Church in Colorado. Just 50 miles from the notorious Columbine High School in Littleton, an intruder armed with hundreds of rounds of ammunition and smoke grenades entered the megachurch and opened fire. He was confronted and killed by former law enforcement officer Jeanne Assam, who was acting as volunteer security for the day. (Although the media and even Assam herself continue to define her role as law enforcement, her legal capacity that day was as a private citizen.)

Why don't armed citizens stop mass shootings? Because they stopped them before they became mass shootings. Would guns in Charleston have stopped the killer? Thanks to lawmakers, we'll never know. However, one thing is clear: Status quo isn't the answer.

Naturally, proponents of non-violence will argue that turning the other cheek takes precedence over protection of the flock. Each must act according to the dictates of his or her conscience, but there's no clear-cut argument that any major world religion demands absolute pacifism. For example, most scholars of Hinduism suggest that the non-violent doctrine of ahimsa does not require ignoring threats to life or limb. Islam resoundingly endorses self-defense. Sikhs carry ceremonial weapons called Kirpans to symbolize courage, self-defense and readiness. Hebrew Scriptures include fairly detailed outlines for the use of deadly force.

The Dalai Lama famously wrote, "If someone has a gun and is trying to kill you, it would be reasonable to shoot back with your own gun." Although personally opposing violence, Mohandas Gandhi condemned laws that disarmed his people from fighting for independence. Moreover, Christian scriptures include an account of Jesus telling his disciples to buy swords, as well as descriptions of a Second Coming when his sword will slay enemy combatants.

In early American history, churches were vital to communities, and each settler was expected to do his part to protect the parishioners from attack. Many colonial settlements levied fines against worshipers for coming to church services with defective or absent firearms. Church lawns were often the scene for Sunday afternoon competitions and tournaments to sharpen the skills of colonialists.

Readers interested in beefing up church security need to check local laws on church carry. Make sure your church isn't acting as a day care or a school. Promote a dialog among the church and clergy. Network with other worshipers to form plans. Periodically volunteer to stand watch outside the service. Greeters and ushers often join services and leave church foyers completely unwatched, allowing open access to would-be perpetrators. Learn to watch for concerning behaviors. Train for worst-case scenarios.

Whatever day and in whatever way, many readers keep the Sabbath. It's not a question of if, but when and where. When preventative measures fail, being caught without the means to defend yourself, even in a house of worship, is a mistake you might only get to make once.

8 CHAPTER EIGHT

But the Lord is faithful, and he will strengthen and protect you from the evil one.

2 THESSALONIANS 3:3

Drones serve hundreds or maybe thousands of useful purposes. Here are a few agencies or companies that employ drones:

- Governments
- Military
- Prisons and detention facilities
- Fire departments
- Law enforcement
- National parks
- Airports

- Sporting venues
- Houses of worship
- Executive protection companies
- Utilities
- Safety companies
- Media

EXAMPLE DRONE INCIDENTS

January 2015
Mexico, U.S. Border

A drone carrying more than 6 pounds of crystal meth crashed in a supermarket parking lot in Tijuana. The DEA commented, "Drones are becoming a common means to transport drugs over the border."

August 2018
Caracas, Venezuela

Drones attacked President Nicolas Maduro while he was giving a speech to the National Guard. His wife and military dignitaries were on stage while hundreds of troops were in formation in front of the stage. Reports indicate that a drone carrying explosives detonated in the air above the soldiers. A second drone exploded seconds later. A third drone crashed into an apartment building where a resident said it broke a window and injured a young girl. Authorities arrested some members of the press along with other suspects. Maduro accused a former military head who fled the country. Officials apprehended the man in January 2019, when he returned to Venezuela.

MILITARY DRONES

Research indicates that the military, in conjunction with the CIA, has been using surveillance drones over Afghanistan since 2000. Armed drones, also called Unmanned Aerial Vehicles (UAVs), were first flown after the 9/11 attacks. In 2002, the United States used a Hellfire missile from a drone to target a leader with close ties to Osama bin Laden. Locals in the area said the missile killed only civilians at a scrapyard. A Pentagon representative refuted the locals, saying that the target was a legitimate military target.

Since 2002, thousands of drones have deployed bombs and missiles in the fight against terrorism. Recent technological advances make smaller drones viable for military use. The government has awarded a $39.6 million U.S. Army contract to produce drones so small they will fit in the palm of a soldier's hand. These drones will perform reconnaissance and surveillance. The Army has dubbed it the Black Hornet Personal Reconnaissance System.

CIVILIAN DRONES

Civilians currently own hundreds of thousands of drones throughout the U.S. The Federal Aviation Administration (FAA) estimates that the number will increase to 2.9 million by 2022. If you own a drone that weighs 0.55 pounds or less and operate it for non-commercial use, you are considered a recreational user. The FAA rules state you must register your drone with their agency if it weighs more than 0.55 pounds, even if you are a recreational user. Non-registered recreational flyers may be subject to state regulations in addition to federal laws. Some states now require all drones to be registered. The following are examples of state laws:

- **Indiana:** Does not allow sex offenders to capture pictures, videos or audible recordings of people while using a drone.

- **New Jersey:** Prohibits anyone from intentionally creating a condition which endangers the safety or security of a correctional facility by operating an unmanned aircraft system on the premises of or near that facility.

- **Montana:** Prohibits anyone from flying a drone over fire suppression efforts at a wildfire. The operator may face fines equal to the cost of the disruption.

- **Connecticut:** Does not allow municipalities to regulate drones.

- **Oregon:** Classifies the weaponization of a drone as a felony. Penalties increase if the weapon injures people.

FAA RULES

The FAA has published rules for drones under the Small Unmanned Aircraft Regulations (Part 107). The rules cover uses for drones weighing 0.55 pounds to 55 pounds. Visit www.gov/uas/ to learn what rules apply to all drones and how to register your drone for commercial use. If you meet the criteria to register your drone and do not do so, you are subject to civil and criminal penalties. To operate a small drone (UAS) for commercial or governmental use, under Part 107, you need a remote pilot certificate with a small UAS rating. You must pass an FAA-approved test at an approved FAA site.

- **Partial List of Commercial Rules**

  o Keep your drone within unaided sight. Binoculars are prohibited.

  o Maximum allowable altitude is 400 feet above the ground except in controlled airspace.

  o Maximum speed is 100 mph.

  o You must register your drone.

  o A certified UAS pilot must operate the drone.

  o You can carry an external load provided the total weight of the drone and cargo does not exceed 55 pounds. State laws may differ.

  o You may request a waiver on specific requirements of Part 107 through the FAA.

- **Partial List of Recreational Rules**

  o The drone must not be used for commercial or governmental use.

  o Never fly higher than 400 feet except as authorized in controlled airspace.

  o Do not fly within 5 miles of an airport unless you receive permission from the control tower of the airport.

  o Never fly over groups of people, public events or stadiums full of people.

  o You may not fly over events such as Major League Baseball games, National Football League games, college football games or NASCAR and Indy Car races.

OPPORTUNITIES FOR HOUSES OF WORSHIP

While working for a church, I had a chance to attend a weeklong event with hundreds of high school students and adult chaperones on a beach in Florida. Other ministries also sent people to work with the students. Besides the security concerns, they tasked me with medical and safety issues. Our communications department sent a drone with an operator. Before leaving our home church, I asked the operator to register the drone with the FAA, which he did. I also reiterated that he may not fly over the crowd. He agreed. He came to me the first day we were on the beach complaining that whenever he tried to fly over the hotel toward the city, the drone stopped, hovered and would not move forward. We learned that the drone had hit a geofence set up by the FAA 5 miles from the local airport. A requested variance from the FAA might have allowed him to fly within the 5-mile perimeter.

Our church held a church-wide event framing sections of homes, loading them on trailers, and sending them to a hurricane-ravaged area of the Gulf Coast for the construction of new homes. Three thousand people showed up and worked for three hours in our parking lot. It was a fantastic day with more than 30 houses framed. The church wanted to record the event to be shown at worship services the following weekend. We employed video cameras, a drone and a videographer in a helicopter to capture the footage. Even though the aircraft flew outside of the crowd, his low altitude caused concern for many people, so I asked him to leave. I also noticed the drone flying over the group, so I spoke to the operator and asked that the drone stay outside the perimeter of the parking lot, no matter its altitude.

Houses of worship employ drones to monitor traffic and help with parking lot security. Drones can also record promotional videos, churchwide events, mission trips, sermon illustrations, worship backgrounds and more. Could your drone be used to augment security for a visiting VIP or dignitary? Before you put the drone in the air, register it with the FAA and ask for any variances in advance of a planned event. Before flying a drone over your property, the operator should notify security and any other departments that need to know.

EXAMPLE DRONE INCIDENTS

December 2018
Gatwick Arport, England

Two drones were seen flying close to a runway within the perimeter of the airport at about 9 p.m. Authorities closed the airport until noon the next day; however, security spotted another drone, which caused another closure. The shutdown stranded 11,000 passengers inside the airport. Another 100,000 passengers had their flights disrupted arriving and departing from Gatwick for the next few days. Two people were arrested but later released.

January 2019
Newark Liberty International Airport

Newark International was closed for about two hours after two pilots on different planes spotted a drone as they came in for landings. One of the pilots said that the drone came within 30 feet of his wing while flying at about 3,500 feet. The FAA reports that they receive more than 100 drone sightings each month from pilots.

CONCERNS FOR HOUSES OF WORSHIP

Could a drone be used as surveillance to gather information for a person or group planning an attack against a house of worship? What about delivering explosives to a target on your premises? How easy would it be to hover next to an entrance, fly into the building when someone opens a door and then detonate an explosive inside your building? What protection do you have against drone operators taking pictures and videos of children playing in your playground and then sharing the images online for nefarious purposes? These are just a few ways drones could hurt your congregation.

A church security director reported finding a drone on the ground close to one of the doors. It apparently had run out of power and fallen. Fortunately, no one was hurt. When he reached out to the FAA, they asked if the drone had a registration number. If so, they would contact the owner and take care of the matter. If not, the security director would have to identify the operator and report him/her to the police. Police would issue a warning, and if the drone flew over the property again, the operator could face trespassing charges.

ANTI-DRONE TECHNOLOGY

Companies across the world are moving quickly to improve existing technology and develop new methods to stop drones. I learned of one such company that does work for the military, sporting venues, prisons and concert promoters. Before a sizable outdoor night concert, the company approached the show's promoter to propose a system that would block drones from flying over the crowd. The promoter declined their offer saying that he couldn't imagine any drones flying at night over the concert. The anti-drone company recorded more than a dozen drones flying over the crowd during the evening. No doubt they were filming the show, but what if one of them carried explosives?

Government agencies and the military work aggressively to combat intrusive drones. Companies connected with the military have passed some of that experiential information to the civilian market. Here are some of the options:

- Geofencing — setting a perimeter that protects an area from drone flight
- Jamming software

- Remote software that can track a drone and locate the operator
- Taking control of the drone from a remote location by overriding the original operator's commands
- Anti-drone drones that collide with the invading drone
- Cannons that fire a net at the drone
- Trained eagles to intercept the drones

WHERE TO FIND HELP

Drone conferences allow experts and manufacturers to share information and display new products. I suggest that you attend one of the more than 100 conferences held annually. Here are the most attended conferences in the U.S.:

- The Consumer Electronics Show
- Drone Expo International
- Commercial UAV Expo
- GEO Business
- AUVSI Xponential
- International Conference on Unmanned Aircraft Systems
- International Security Conference & Exposition
- American Society for Industrial Security (ASIS) Security Conference & Expo

EXAMPLE DRONE INCIDENTS

February 2019
Atlanta, Georgia

Federal officials confiscated six unauthorized drones as they flew over the Super Bowl site in Atlanta three days before the big game. The FAA restricted drones within 1 nautical mile of the stadium. That ban was stretched out to 30 nautical miles starting 30 minutes before the game and ending at midnight. A violator could serve time in jail and face a fine of up to $20,000. Law enforcement and military helicopters flew over the site before, during and after the game. Military F-16s patrolled at higher altitudes.

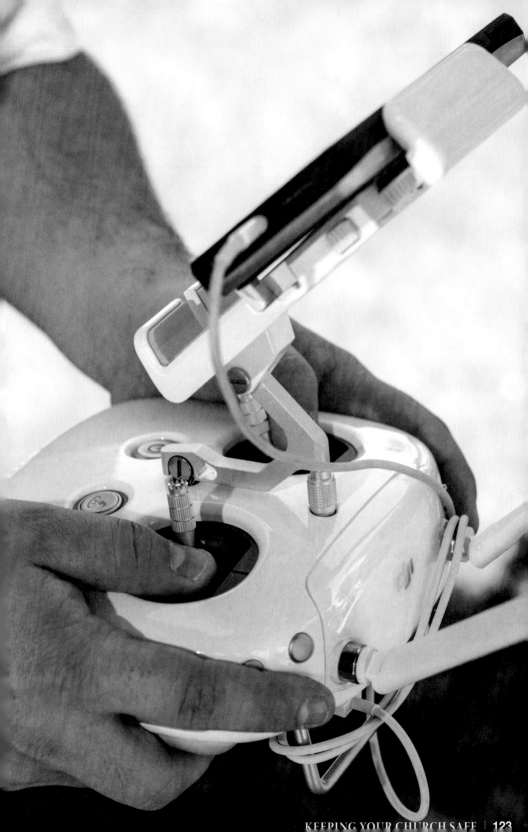

9 CHAPTER NINE

- Church Protesters
- Protests
- People of Concern
- Other Incidents

But the chief priests stirred up the crowd to have Pilate release Barabbas instead.

MARK 1:11 (NIV)

PROTESTS

On occasion, a group that does not align with the teachings of a house of worship may decide to protest. This group may have connections with national organizations that promote issues such as pro-choice, same-sex marriage, white nationalism, etc. They are well organized and well funded. Some organizations may even pay people to protest.

EXAMPLE CHURCH PROTESTERS

- A small Kansas church sent protesters to a large sporting event two states away to proclaim with signs that God hated homosexuals. While in town, they also protested in front of three large Christian churches on Sunday morning. They carried signs stating, "Your Pastor Is Lying," and "God's Judgment Is Upon You." Protesters, who included women and young children, harassed arriving churchgoers by yelling derogatory remarks.

- The men's group at a church held a "wild game feed." Hunters within the church donated meat from their kills and were encouraged to invite friends who may not belong to a church. After the meal, the church gave any leftovers to a local charity. The evening's agenda included a time of music and a message following the dinner. During the meal, a man dressed as Jesus entered the dining hall proclaiming it was a sin to eat meat and that killing animals is cruel and inhumane.

- A church allowed a para-church organization to host a conference at its facility. During the opening meeting of the conference, a few protesters stood in the audience, unfurled a banner, then yelled insults at the speaker. Officials escorted the demonstrators out of the building.

- In the middle of a Christmas Eve service message, a young man in the congregation stood and yelled proclaiming that the church was not doing enough for the poor and hungry in the community. Off-duty police officers removed the disruptor from the building and arrested him for disorderly conduct.

Similarly, local issues can trigger protests. For example, let's say your church wants to expand and purchase adjoining land. Local officials call for a public hearing, and to your surprise, people show up to voice their opposition to the plan. They say that you are already too big and expanding will only cause traffic problems and unwanted nighttime activities. You might see them on a Sunday morning carrying signs of protest in front of your church.

Response to Protests

- Large municipalities may require a permit to protest. Initiate a standing request that the permit-issuing agency and your local police notify your office when they grant licenses for protests near your church.

- Never allow protesters on your property. Ask the police to stand by during the protest, and if someone comes on your property, ask the police to assist you and inform the protester(s) that he or she must leave your property. If the person refuses, press trespassing charges. I would suggest you talk to the police before the protest starts to determine what you can and cannot do. The general rule is that protesters can walk on public property, such as a sidewalk or in front of your property but are not allowed to slow or impede vehicular or pedestrian traffic. Again, this is a police matter and the police should handle this.

- The same rules apply for protesters in a meeting. You can ask them to sit and be quiet. If they refuse, you then ask them to leave. If they refuse to go, charge them with trespassing. In some jurisdictions, laws exist to protect large assemblies of people. If someone gets up and shouts during a meeting or worship service, he or she is committing a crime.

- Consider hiring off-duty police officers. In a small church, you may ask a member who is a law enforcement officer to volunteer. The investment is a wise one, especially if something should happen.

- A couple of churches that I know have sent representatives to meet with leaders of the protest organizations the day before planned protests. Both occasions involved holding conferences at the churches. One church felt that it was essential to meet with the protesters to dispel any myths and to answer any questions. The second church met with the protest leaders and did much of the same. In fact, after the meeting, the church set up a couple of portable restrooms on the edge of the property to be used by the protesters. They also delivered bottled water to the group on the day of the event. Both churches reached out in the name of Christ. No arrests were made, and conference meetings carried on with no interruptions at both sites.

PEOPLE OF CONCERN

Active shooters garner much focus, as it should be, but churches deal with domestic disturbances, the mentally ill and other interpersonal conflicts on a much more frequent basis. Every situation is different. Here are a few tips to consider when reacting to a disturbance in your house of worship:

- **Bring help.** If possible, have someone with you. Bring a female if the person is female.
- **Stay calm.** Your demeanor should reflect control and a willingness to listen. Do not be condescending or aggressive.

EXAMPLE OTHER INCIDENTS

- On Mother's Day Sunday, during the sound check for morning worship, a man walked into the worship center wearing only a bathrobe and underwear. Security attempted to talk to him but could not reason with him. As EMS was placing him in the ambulance for transport to a hospital for psychiatric evaluation, his mother showed up and said he was having problems.

- A 25-year-old male came in to speak to the "head man" to tell him that God had told him he was the new senior minister. EMS transported him to a hospital for a 72-hour psychiatric evaluation. An hour after he was released, he came back to the church. They charged him with criminal trespassing. With consultation from a church representative, the judge released the man, instructing him to not return to the church.

- At 9 a.m. Monday, a couple asked to speak to a pastor. The couple asked the pastor for money to travel out of state to attend a relative's funeral. If that was not possible, they requested a hotel room for the night. The church paid for their hotel room. The next morning, the hotel manager called to complain that the couple had stolen numerous items from the room, including the comforter that covered the bed.

- **Assess the situation.** Is the person agitated, angry or calm?
- **Ask questions.** Don't be judgmental. Find out what's going on before deciding how to respond. When dealing with the homeless, ask for a name and try to learn more about the individual. Ask if they're carrying a weapon. A homeless person will typically carry a knife or have a dog for protection. Rarely will they have a gun.
- **Try to understand the why.** Be aware that the individual may have a grudge against the church or may be mentally unstable.
- **Use cautious interaction.** Do not invade the trespasser's personal space unless it is necessary. Be careful with how and when you place hands on the individual. Call the police when necessary. Don't wait.

- A father attempted to pick up his child from a church's child care ministry during Sunday worship. He told the volunteer he had a right to pick up the child but could not produce the child's tag. The volunteer notified a supervisor and, during discussion, learned that the father was divorced from the child's mom and did not have the legal authority to pick the child up. The father became frustrated, threw his coffee at the supervisor and left. Fortunately, the coffee was not hot.

- A woman asked to speak to security on a Sunday morning. She produced an Emergency Protective Order against her ex-husband saying he must not have contact with her and was required to stay at least 1,000 feet away from her. She said she saw him in the building.

- A divorced couple argued while exchanging children under a church portico. The ex-husband became angry and threatened his ex-wife. His actions became more aggressive and, fearing for her safety, the woman left. She filed a motion in court, subpoenaed security footage from the camera viewing the portico and required a security team member to testify at the family court hearing on the authenticity of the recording.

- A man appearing to be homeless walked into the church during Sunday service asking for money and food.

10 CHAPTER TEN

Whether you're collecting $100 or $10,000 during a weekend, prioritize the safety of everyone in your building. Most churches publish the amount of last week's offering in the bulletin. Such public announcements could entice a criminal to commit robbery or theft after reading your bulletin. Your job is to present a visible front that will dissuade these individuals. If you are using off-duty uniformed officers to direct traffic, bring them in to escort the offering to the safe or the bank. Strategically locate the officers to observe and protect.

EXAMPLE STOLEN MONEY

- A large church had the weekend offering of more than $150,000 stolen. Most of the total consisted of personal checks, but there was also $7,000 in cash. According to police, an authorized staff person gave the money to a man dressed as a courier. Later that day, the real courier arrived to pick up the cash and checks.

- A church business manager was arrested for embezzlement after he was caught stealing $58,000 from the church where he worked.

- The chief financial officer of a church stole $850,000 from the church. A judge sentenced him to eight years in prison.

- A security guard and his friend were caught on surveillance cameras breaking into the basement of a church and unlocking a safe over four consecutive weekends. The security guard was a church employee. The theft totaled approximately $100,000.

BEST PRACTICES

- Count the bags/plates going in and coming out of the worship center during the collection of offerings.

- After collection, escort the money to a private room that is guarded by an off-duty officer or an armed security team member. Bag the money in this private room.

- If you use an offering box, secure it so it's not easily carried out or breached.

- Have an armored car service take the money to the bank. If this is not feasible, request a police escort to the bank.

- When contracting with an armored car service, insist that a marked company vehicle with two guards make the pickup. Most companies place a hidden bar code reader in your building that is scanned by the guard before money is handed over. Also check the guard's ID card, which should be displayed on the uniform, when he or she arrives.

- Have an independent auditing firm do an annual audit.

- Run a criminal background check and credit history report on anyone handling money. Use the company that does your background checks for children's volunteers.

ALTERNATIVES

- Escort money to the church's safe. You should choose a drop safe and bolt it to the floor.

- A security camera and alarm should monitor the room which houses the safe.

- If counting the money on Monday, provide security.

- Provide police protection for the Monday run to the bank. Vary your leave times.

SAFES

During a church consultation, I visited the accounting office. A drop safe, about 3 feet tall and 2 feet wide, sat on the counter in the office. The safe was not bolted down, so a strong person could have picked it up and walked out with it. It was also in plain view from the visitor counter in the room next door. After discussion, they concealed the safe in a lower cabinet. They also bolted the safe to the floor.

On another consultation trip, I noticed that the church kept the weekend offering in rolling armored cases and stored the cases in the locked accounting office. Although the door was locked, the ceiling in the hallway and the office had drop ceilings that would allow a criminal to access the office quite easily. At that point, he could then push the wheeled carts outside to a waiting truck. There were no security cameras.

There are a variety of uses for a safe in your church. You could use it to hold the offering before counting, for the Wednesday night meal money or for registration money for sporting events or Bible class. First, determine the need, then the size and location of the safe. Here are a few recommendations:

- Buy a safe that you can bolt to the floor.
- If you can afford it, purchase a safe with an electronic keypad. The combination should be changed at least every six months.
- Do not place the safe in view of people walking by or from a public area.
- Protect the safe room with a security camera and monitored alarm.
- Purchase your safe from a locksmith, not a local department store. Remember, you get what you pay for.

Large or megachurches may need more than one safe. A hidden drop safe at the welcome center or reception desk could handle middle-of-the week offering drops and registrations. A larger safe that holds the untallied offering could be in a protected room elsewhere. Some megachurches even have walk-in vaults. These vaults also house a large drop safe that keeps the weekend offering until it is counted or picked up by armored car.

11) CHAPTER ELEVEN

But if anyone causes one of these little ones who believe in me to sin, it would be better for him to have a large millstone hung around his neck and to be drowned in the depths of the sea.

MATTHEW 18:6 (NIV)

- Pennsylvania, 2012 — A former pastor faced 200 counts of sexual abuse with 20 known victims. The courts sentenced him to a minimum of 30 years in prison.

- Alabama, 2014 — A former children's minister was charged with 36 counts of abuse and sentenced to 30 years in prison. The abuse occurred on church-sponsored trips, at camp retreats, in his office, during sleepovers at his home and in a church van.

- Maryland, 2014 — A former church youth minister received 40 years in prison for sexually abusing six boys that he met at church and in a Christian school.

- The United Kingdom, 2016 — Authorities arrested a 30-year-old male for 91 known abuse charges spanning eight years. He received 22 life sentences. The perpetrator posed as a Christian English teacher willing to teach youth in impoverished communities in Kuala Lumpur, Malaysia.

The cases in the breakout above all deal with sexual abuse, which is where most of this chapter will focus. However, according to the director of a children's hospital, physical abuse is reported more often than sexual abuse. It is imperative that your church takes reasonable steps to prevent all forms of child abuse and other crimes against children. Seek training from your local Crimes Against Children unit of your police department and from medical professionals trained to spot abuse.

When Jesus walked the earth, he was very clear how important children were to him. In the book of Mark (NIV), Chapter 9, verse 37, he says, "Whoever welcomes one of these little children in my name welcomes me;" and in verse 42, he says, "And if anyone causes one of these little ones who believe in me to sin, it would be better for him to be thrown into the sea with a large millstone tied around his neck."

Types of Child Abuse

- Sexual
- Physical
- Emotional
- Neglect
- Ritual

SEXUAL ABUSE

Attorney Greg Love of MinistrySafe defines sexual abuse as: "Any tricked, forced, manipulated or coerced sexual activity for the pleasure of the abuser (physical, verbal or visual)."

Greg and his team at MinistrySafe have fought, and continue to fight, child abuse through training, teaching and consultations. MinistrySafe has a program specifically designed for houses of worship.

Facts:

- Studies indicate that as many as one in four females and one in six males face sexual abuse by the time they reach 18 years of age.
- More than 90 percent of abusers are known and trusted by their victims. This includes family, friends, coaches, etc.
- Most abuse takes place by someone who has created a relationship with the child through "grooming." The abuser will also "groom" the child's parents or caregivers.
- "Grooming" does not need to take place if the victim is a very young child. The abuser needs only opportunity.
- The typical offender is between 20 and 30 years of age.
- The average abusive male begins abusing at 13 or 14 years of age.
- Eighty-five percent of convicted offenders are married and have children.
- When arrested, adults who molested boys averaged 150 victims.
- When arrested, adults who molested girls averaged 52 victims.
- Ninety percent of abusers are male.
- Many victims do not report abuse.

Reporting Requirements

All 50 states have reporting requirements for child sexual abuse. Some are very narrow while others are broad; but the bottom line is, if you have knowledge or suspicion of abuse, report it. You may be criminally liable if you don't. Every state and most cities have an office to call, such as Child Protective Services. If the abuse is life-threatening, notify local law enforcement immediately. The safety of a child may depend on you.

SIGNS OF SEXUAL ABUSE

When a child is sexually abused, he or she will often show some of the following signs:

- Depression
- Promiscuity
- Sexual diseases
- Physical ailments
- Outbursts of anger
- Self-abuse

Sexual abuse trauma manifests itself in different ways. Younger children tend to become self-absorbed and may try to hurt themselves. In most cases, the child will have physical problems in the area of the body violated during the crime. Older children may become sexually active and display inappropriate behavior for their ages. They may be unable to hold their emotions in check and could have outbursts of anger. For example, a child who used to be outgoing and affectionate now refuses to let an adult touch them or even get close.

Grooming

Grooming is the process by which an abuser draws a victim into a sexual relationship and maintains that relationship in secrecy.

Abusers will profile children while seeking their victims. They usually have age and gender preferences. In most cases, before the abuse occurs, they must gain the trust of the victim or anyone that is a protector of the victim, such as his/her parents, coaches or family friends. Physical contact with the child will start slowly and then progress as boundaries are pushed, testing limits and gaining trust. The abuser might offer to babysit or take the child on an overnight trip, such as camping, a concert or a sporting event. The trips may start as group outings, shrinking the group until the abuser is alone with the child. He'll lie to the adults around the child saying that these trips involve many children, when, in fact, it may be only one or two. He'll tell the child to keep it a secret by offering gifts or introducing "adult" things to the child. Pornography, money, alcohol or drugs are often used to entice boys; girls are often bribed with flowers, candy, alcohol, drugs or money. The abuser maintains control by withholding these items or by threatening physical harm or exposure of the child's behavior.

The abuser will often identify a child who seems unpopular, unloved, has low self-confidence and has little parental oversight. As children age from elementary to middle school, they form groups or cliques. The abuser will search out the child on the fringe of these groups — the one

who doesn't fit in. It bears mentioning that in ministry, these children are purposefully sought out by pastors and ministers. In these cases, adults reach out to the children to bring them back into the larger group, even spending one-on-one time with them. However, these interactions must be done in public and with knowledge and oversight by other ministry team members.

Social media can be a big part of grooming, as well. The abuser may pose as another child, even changing his gender to match that of his victim. He will bring up sexual topics that can lead to exchanging inappropriate pictures. When the abuser feels the time is right, he'll ask for a face-to-face meeting. At the meeting, the abuser will often gain control of the child by showing the texts and pictures sent to him and threatening to share them.

TIPS FOR PARENTS

Share these tips with parents and caregivers of children that attend your house of worship and attend your programs. Extend the knowledge to protect our children.

- Teach children the difference between a safe and unsafe secret.

- You must have access to your child's phone and computer. Learn how to identify software that the child may have installed to prevent access to his or her messaging.

- No adult friend of the family should be allowed to text your child without copying you. This includes church staff and adult volunteers.

- Do not allow an adult to be alone with your child. No car rides, going to the movies, rides home, etc. Again, this includes church staff as well as coaches and other adult leaders.

- Teach children to respect authority, but they need to know they have the right to say "NO" or "STOP!"

- Permit them to tell you about anything not "normal" in their life. This is anything that makes them feel uneasy or weird when certain people get around them.

- Peer-on-peer abuse is real. Learn how to spot it and always provide adequate supervision. Sometimes consensual activities elevate to abuse.

TIPS FOR HOUSES OF WORSHIP

- The two-adult rule includes dropping children off using a church vehicle or private car after a church function.

- Train all staff and children's volunteers on sexual abuse prevention.

- Install security cameras in all children's classrooms and hallways.

- Have automatic light switches in all classrooms and adequate night lights in hallways.

- Never be out of view of others when talking to a child. No closed-door counseling sessions or private meetings should occur.

- Learn what peer-on-peer abuse is and how to recognize it.

- Follow adult-child ratios. Never deviate. When setting ratios, check with your state agency in charge of regulating day care centers. At the least, follow the minimum ratios.

- Do not allow pictures or video to be taken of children unless authorized by parents.

- Check with your insurance company to learn if you have coverage for acts of child sexual abuse occurring on your property and during church-sponsored activities. Inform them of any prevention programs you have in place.

PHYSICAL ABUSE

As a child care provider for weekend worship and weekday child care, you must be trained in recognizing physical abuse. A pattern of bruises may indicate physical abuse. These bruises may be on different parts of the body but will show up consistently, week after week. The child may display cuts and burns in much the same way. Facial injuries may be less consistent but more disturbing. Self-abuse may occur, such as pulling hair or hitting themselves. They may also have an outburst of anger and might fear to be around adults.

Signs of Physical Abuse:

- Bruises
- Cuts
- Burns
- Facial injuries
- Self-abuse
- Anger
- Fearful of adults

NEGLECT

A person may be guilty of negligence by not providing the basic needs of a child, such as food, safe shelter, clean clothes, affection or even medical care.

Signs of Neglect:

- Depression
- Poor hygiene
- Persistent hunger
- Food hoarding
- Shoplifting/stealing

EMOTIONAL ABUSE

Children may be threatened with violence or regularly told they are worthless and unloved. They may be forced to commit crimes out of fear or because they are seeking affirmation and love.

Signs of Emotional Abuse:

- Depression
- Suicidal suggestions or actions
- Passive-aggressive behavior
- Eating disorders

RITUAL ABUSE

Someone in charge of their well-being controls the child. It may be a guardian or even a parent. Their actions are justified by a "higher" power, which might be the head of a religious group or cult. The child can be forced to perform illegal or immoral acts with someone or a group of people.

Types of Ritual Abuse:

- Animal cruelty
- Sexual abuse
- Physical abuse
- Emotional abuse

RESPONSIBILITY

Prepare for the unexpected. Train your staff and volunteers to recognize the symptoms and signs of abuse. If you suspect abuse, report it to your supervisor and the authorities. Start an investigation and keep a written record. Also, contact your attorney and insurance agent. Verify that someone has notified the child's parents. If a staff member, volunteer or church member faces allegations of impropriety, remove the suspect from his or her position. Although the circle of notification seems large, information shared must remain confidential.

Appoint a media representative in case the media learns of the allegations. In most cases, this will not be the pastor. He might be emotionally involved and may say something that could incriminate the church or that might jeopardize the investigation. Your representative should always consult with the authorities in charge before making any statements.

A few years ago, a representative of a church called me for advice on setting up a security program. We discussed many things, including the importance of doing criminal background checks. He implemented this along with some other suggestions. About six months later, he called again. A minister working in his youth ministry faced charges of soliciting sex from a minor when he tried to meet a 14-year-old girl with whom he had been chatting online. It turned out that the girl was, in fact, a detective with a local police department. The story had been published, along with the minister's picture in the morning newspaper. He did the following after consulting with me, the senior pastor and an attorney:

- One of the church's ministers met with the accused, who was in jail.

- A media representative was appointed. He held discussions with the church's attorney and the police before the media arrived.

- A congregational meeting was called within a couple of days to denounce the occurrence, to explain steps the church had taken up to that point and to outline future measures to prevent such a thing from happening again.

- An ad in the local paper announced a public meeting at the church for any interested parties. At the well-attended meeting, a question-and-answer session followed the reading of a prepared statement.

The church had performed criminal background and reference checks on the youth minister before hiring him. His record was clean and all references were excellent. The members and public needed to know this.

SUMMARY OF CHILD ABUSE

- **Prepare:** Train your staff and volunteers on how to identify abuse and how and when to report it.

- **Respond:** Immediately investigate any allegation of abuse or possible abuse. If a medical professional is on site, have them accompany you. Try to confirm the report through interviews and observations.

- **Notify:** Always err on the side of caution and report to the authorities if you feel something may have happened. Call the church's attorney and church leadership. If you think that the abuse does not involve the parents or guardians, call them as well.

- **Provide Help:** If appropriate, provide help to the child and family.

VOLUNTEERS

Most churches could not function without volunteers. The focus of this section will be on volunteers who work with children. Although you may struggle to get enough volunteers for the children's ministry, do not accept just anyone. I remember working in the restaurant business when we were very short-handed. The supervisor said that the only qualifications needed for a new hire were that they were standing and breathing. You may be tempted to do the same. Don't! Always screen your workers before they work with children.

Take a colored "head and shoulders" photo of your new volunteer and place it in his or her personnel folder. Require that all volunteers be at least 18 years of age. Teenage junior helpers may assist, but they can never be in charge.

Every church must utilize a set of minimum requirements for children's volunteers. Criminal background checks are good, but they are not enough. Here is a list of eight requirements that will help you start the placement process for a new volunteer.

❶ **Waiting Period** — Do not allow someone to volunteer with children the first week they attend your church. Every church must have a waiting period. Abusers want quick, easy access to children. I would recommend three months as a minimum. Large or megachurches should have a six-month waiting period. You'll have to decide whether you will allow non-members or members only to volunteer. Either way, verify their attendance. Do not take their word for it.

❷ **Background Check** — Use a reputable company. Ask your insurance agent and other churches for recommendations. Do a national criminal background search and a national sex offender registry search. I've known insurance companies to require checks every three years. Some federal agencies say every five years is reasonable. I liked running them every two years. You'd be surprised by what I found. Appoint one person to review all criminal checks. Preferably this person will have a law enforcement or legal background. He or she will be able to decipher and understand court records on the background check.

If a report comes back that disqualifies an applicant, call the applicant to verify the charge and to notify them of the disqualification. This will not be a surprise as he or she received a copy of the criminal check you ran. In most cases, the applicant understands that there are consequences for the actions, even though he or she has joined the church or committed his or her life to Christ. Then lock the applicant's information away from other staff and volunteers. It must be kept confidential.

There is always a question of what crimes disqualify an applicant. My advice is to treat each person separately. However, under no circumstances should anyone with a history of violent or sexual crimes be allowed to work with children.

❸ **Reference Check** — I recommend asking for three references: a relative, a co-worker and a friend. Contact all of them and do not place the volunteer until all three respond. Even though the applicant gives the names, you may receive surprising feedback.

❹ **Applicant Interview** — Have a face-to-face interview. No phone interviews.

❺ **Sexual Abuse Prevention Training** — Train every volunteer in this area.

❻ **Policies and Procedures** — Go over policies and procedures aimed at the age group with which the volunteer will be working. This will include safety as well as security protocols. Keep records of all training.

❼ **First Aid, CPR, AED Training** —
Your local Red Cross office or any certified instructor can conduct training. Large or megachurches can certify one staff member who then is responsible for the preparation of volunteers.

❽ **Shadowing / Supervision** —
It's a good idea to have the new volunteer shadow someone for two or three weekends. Monitor all volunteers on an ongoing basis.

VOLUNTEER RESPONSIBILITIES

- Attend a mandatory training session that includes child care procedures, when and whom to call for help, conflict resolution, sexual abuse prevention and any other training the church deems necessary.

- Notify the volunteer's supervisor and the authorities if child abuse is suspected.

- Never release a child to an unauthorized person. Nobody can take a child from a room without a matching security tag. Child recognition does not count since a child would recognize either parent in a divorce situation. A staff member or volunteer supervisor should be called by the in-room volunteer when there is a question.

- Be observant for safety hazards, discipline problems and adults wandering the halls without children.

- Express love and care in appropriate ways. Avoid kissing a child or touching a child in an area that would be covered by a bathing suit, except when changing a diaper or assisting in a restroom. Do this in the presence of another adult. Avoid frequently carrying children older than infants or toddlers or having them sit on your lap.

- Never permit anyone to take pictures of children unless it is someone that the church has approved and only after obtaining permission from the child's parents.

PARENTAL RESPONSIBILITIES

- Receive and review a copy of the church's safety and security handout/attend an orientation class about policies and procedures of the children's area.

- Indicate on the registration form who has permission to drop off and pick up the child. Take a photo of the parent and child and place it in the child's church folder.

- Provide copies of any court documents if there is a separation or divorce. This eliminates any arguments or confrontations when the child is dropped off or picked up.

- Report any suspicious or unusual behavior in the children's area to a staff member or volunteer. Examples would be a child wandering alone or an adult who seems "out of place."

- Follow procedures for drop-off and pickup. Sending an unauthorized friend or a minor sibling to pick up the child because you are busy is prohibited. Be the example, not the exemption.

SEX OFFENDERS

What do you do when a sex offender wants to attend your church? Churches differ significantly in opinions. Some say never; others say yes. A third group says yes, with guidelines. I like the third option. An offender might approach the church and ask to attend or someone in the congregation may tell you they've seen an offender attending.

If the offender asks to attend, I'd have him meet with a pastor and a security team member. First, ask him to provide the name and phone number of his probation or parole officer. If he refuses, ask him to leave and not return. If he does provide the number, call during the meeting. When presented with the circumstances, the officer will approve or disapprove of the offender's attendance. Disapproval is typically the result of non-compliance or a recent release from prison. If passed and you decide to have him attend, I recommend assigning a mentor to him. The mentor will meet him in the parking lot and stay with him while he is at church. He is not allowed to attend any children's activities. If he breaks this agreement with the church, tell him to leave immediately and notify his probation/parole officer.

12 CHAPTER TWELVE

- Environmental Design
- Identifying Staff and Volunteers
- Child Drop-Off and Pickup Procedures
- Adult-Child Ratios
- Crime Prevention
- Missing Children

Whoever welcomes one of these little children in my name welcomes me...

MARK 9:37 (NIV)

ENVIRONMENTAL DESIGN

Use a central point into the children's area so it is easy to monitor everyone entering or exiting the space. In large houses of worship with multiple entry points, post a greeter at each door. If an entry is unmanned, lock it to prevent any unauthorized entry by outsiders with ill intentions. Never chain a door. Exit doors must always be able to be pushed open from the inside in case of an emergency. Install security cameras at all entry points, hallways and classrooms. Do not put cameras in restrooms or nursing rooms.

Keep doors open in classrooms. Install "Dutch" or half doors which will allow visibility and maintain security. If a solid door is used, install a door skylight. Classroom doors must be able to be locked from the inside in case of an emergency lockdown.

IDENTIFYING STAFF AND VOLUNTEERS

Identifying staff and volunteers is as easy as having them wear brightly colored smocks, vests or clothing, along with a picture ID or name tag. One suggestion is for team leaders to wear one color and everyone else another. While smocks work well in the early childhood department, a picture ID alone works in junior and senior high areas.

CHILD DROP-OFF AND PICKUP PROCEDURES

It is a good idea to make a copy of a parent's driver's license and to take a photo of the child and parent(s) when collecting information at the initial check-in.

Personal information to collect includes name, address, phone number, a list of people authorized to pick up and drop off the child and any specific medical information. Many churches now use software programs to collect and store this information. The program also issues personal identification stickers — one to be placed on the child, one given to the parent and another to be used on a diaper bag, if needed. This system also works with clip-on tags. If a parent tries to pick up a child without the tag or sticker, staff should alert a supervisor. The parent may claim that they've lost the sticker, so having photos and other information on file will aid in confirming positive identification and pickup authorization.

I once had a lady attempt to pick up an 11-year-old boy after service. His mother had dropped him off with the understanding that he would be leaving with her friend so he could play with her son. She did not inform the staff, nor did she give her friend the child's sticker. After the team refused to let her have the child, she attempted to sneak the child out through a side door. The staffer called me, but I was not able to reach the child's parents. Even though the child said he knew the lady, I refused to release him. The woman became furious, but I stood my ground and asked her to leave. We fed the boy lunch, and an hour later, his mom answered her cellphone and came by to pick him up. She was most apologetic and thanked us for abiding by our policy.

ADULT-CHILD RATIOS

Check with the state agency responsible for day care licensing when setting adult-child ratios. This will give you a minimum standard with which to work. Take this information to your leadership, attorney and insurance company, to help you decide on what your ratios should be. Once set, do not deviate from them. Here is a recommended adult-child ratio from birth to 17 years of age.

AGE OF CHILDREN	RATIO
Birth – 1 year	1 adult for 3 children
1 to 2 years	1 adult for 6 children
2 to 3 years	1 adult for 10 children
3 to 4 years	1 adult for 12 children
4 to 5 years	1 adult for 14 children
5 to 7 years	1 adult for 15 children
7 to 17 years	1 adult for 25 children

CRIME PREVENTION

All areas, including closets and bathrooms, should be inspected before and after programming. Look for people in unauthorized areas, unattended boxes, packages or bags. If anything is out of place or appears suspicious, report it to the security team immediately. Lock any doors into closets and classrooms not being used during programs. Assign someone to walk around the department while children are there and look for anything unusual or suspicious.

Staff members, volunteers and parents are part of your safety and security "front line." They should report any suspicious activity. This might include an adult walking around alone while classes are in session or someone taking pictures of children or classrooms. Sometimes children will not be well behaved when leaving the church. Pay particular attention to a child that appears to be fearful and is trying to get away from an adult. Check the situation out. Tell someone to watch you when you approach the adult. Don't be embarrassed if everything is OK. Remember to always err on the side of caution.

MISSING CHILDREN

If a child is reported missing, the person who takes the initial report must record information in writing. This would include items like:

- Time the report first comes in
- Person (or people) reporting the missing child
- When and where the child was last seen
- Person or persons who last saw the child
- Description of the child
- Inform the parents (if they are not the ones reporting the missing child)
- Question volunteers to ascertain that the child was not already released

Do NOT rely on your memory. WRITE it down.

- Communicate information to everyone who has a church radio.
- Inform all staff, volunteers, ushers, greeters and parking lot volunteers.
- Station an adult at every exit door.

If the child has gone missing from a classroom, search the room carefully, including closets and cabinets. Children often play hide-and-seek in these areas. Start to widen your search to adjacent classrooms, closets, storage rooms, stairwells, etc. Staff all vehicle entry and exit roads in case you need to close the exits. Stop exiting vehicles and talk to the occupants. This will slow traffic down, giving you time to search your buildings and parking lots. Frequently a lost child will go to the vehicle to wait for his or her parents. If you cannot find the child within a few minutes, call law enforcement and close your exits. Law enforcement officers will search vehicles as people leave. If you have security cameras, review security footage as the search continues.

I once had a 13-year-old girl reported missing by her parents. They related that while they were placing their 5-year-old child in child care between services, they became separated from their older daughter. They searched for her and after 40 minutes, frantically reached out to church security fearful that someone had abducted their daughter. Due to the delay in reporting their daughter missing, I immediately locked down our premises and had every available staff and volunteer searching the main building and youth center. Our second service was about to end, which would release 4,000 people and cause additional problems in locating her. I had our uniformed off-duty officers stop and search every car leaving the property. While this was happening, I reviewed our security footage and identified the family as they dropped off the younger child in our children's wing. The missing teenager was seen intentionally walking away from her family in the crowd. A short while later, we found her among the crowd exiting the worship center. It seemed that she didn't want to attend service and hid in a stairwell. Fortunately, the vehicle exits were blocked for only a few minutes. It was the only time during my 19 years as Safety and Security Director that I closed exits and searched vehicles.

thinking

informal

terrorism

intimi

terrori

Rescue me, O Lord, from evil men; protect me from men of violence, who devise evil plans in their hearts and stir up war every day.

PSALM 140:1-2 (NIV)

This book covers many ways to provide a safe and secure environment at your house of worship. Now I want to focus on terrorism as it pertains to houses of worship in America. Much of what we have covered previously can and should be used as part of an overall safety and security plan; however, you may benefit from additional information about terrorism. I'm not trying to be an alarmist. I just want to provide information that will help in your fight against crime. Consider the following as a starting point. I strongly recommend consulting with your local FBI office, your state's office of Homeland Security and local law enforcement.

We attach the label of "terrorist" to those who resort to violence to perpetuate their cause. What a terrorist looks for when choosing a target is maximum exposure, maximum terror and maximum casualties. Terrorists desire to make the most significant impact, and the possibility of creating publicity rises with the number of people killed or injured in any attack.

"The ruling to kill the Americans and their allies ... civilians and military ... is an individual duty for every Muslim who can do it in any country in which it is possible to do it ... to comply with God's order to kill the Americans and plunder their money wherever and whenever they find it. We also call on Muslim ulema, leaders, youths and soldiers to launch the raid on Satan's U.S. troops and devil's supporters allying with them..."

— Osama bin Laden, Jihad Against Jews and Crusaders, 1998

Sept. 11, 2001, is a date that will live in our memories forever. Thousands of innocent people perished in an attack on the United States. The U.S. immediately went on the offensive. We learned who the hijackers were. Osama bin Laden and al-Qaida became familiar names to us all. We had to adjust our attitudes toward safety, and extra security became the norm. Five short weeks after the attacks, the U.S. government formed the Transportation Security Administration (TSA). The TSA's mission is to prevent similar attacks by assuming primary security responsibility at more than 400 airports.

In addition to creating the TSA, the government moved to protect "high-value targets," such as nuclear power plants, utilities, seaports and military installations. Not included on this list were thousands of houses of worship, hundreds of which have thousands of people attending worship services each weekend.

Many Americans believe that their house of worship is the safest place in town. Many want to believe that an act of terrorism against a congregation, as is regularly seen in other countries, will never happen in the U.S. One could argue that the shooting at the Synagogue in Pennsylvania was an act of terrorism, even though no foreign terrorist group has claimed responsibility. Many experts believe it is just a matter of time before terrorists bring organized attacks against religious groups and houses of worship here in the United States.

October 2001
Bahawalpur, Pakistan

As Christians prayed during a church service, six masked Islamic terrorists with automatic weapons entered the church and opened fire. As they mercilessly killed 15 church members, the terrorists screamed, "Blood for blood!" Press reports said the Christians became victims because of U.S. efforts to capture Osama bin Laden

May 2010
Lahore, Pakistan

Mosques in two neighborhoods faced simultaneous attacks. Attackers entered both mosques, firing their weapons indiscriminately and throwing grenades into the crowds of worshipers. Two bombers blew themselves up at one location, while attackers at another hunted down and killed people for the next two hours. People in the congregation overpowered and captured one perpetrator. The attacks killed 94 and wounded 120. The Pakistan Taliban claimed responsibility.

March 2016
Lahore, Pakistan

Seventy-eight people died and 362 suffered injuries on Easter Sunday when a bomb exploded in one of the largest parks in the city. The attack targeted Christians, but victims also included Muslims who were in the park. A group affiliated with the Pakistan Taliban claimed responsibility.

September 2017
Ancha, Nigeria

Authorities reported that 20 Christians were killed and five injured when Fulani herdsman attacked a village in reprisal for a young Fulani boy who had been slain a year earlier in another town. The attackers shot the victims shortly after midnight while most of the village was asleep.

December 2017
Quetta, Pakistan

Four men attacked the Bethel Memorial Methodist Church during services. Two of the men wore bombs strapped to their bodies. As the bombers attempted to enter the compound, security personnel stationed on the exterior wall and roof of the complex fired on them. One attacker managed to make it to the front door of the worship center where he detonated the bomb vest. Another attacker died and two others fled. The attack claimed 11 lives and injured five.

January 2019
Jolo, Philippines

While worshipers entered Our Lady of Mount Carmel Catholic Cathedral, a bomb exploded in the cathedral. As people ran outside to seek safety, a second bomb exploded in the parking lot. Twenty-seven died and 111 suffered injuries in the explosions. Reports indicate that the Abu Sayyef carried out the bombings and the Islamic State claimed responsibility.

Foreign terrorist groups and U.S. sympathizers know that most churches present soft targets, with little to no security in place. It's very easy to walk into a large church on Sunday with hundreds or thousands in attendance and not be questioned or searched. Ask yourself how easy it would be for someone to walk into your church with a bomb strapped to his chest or carrying a backpack full of explosives. I recently visited a church that publishes a security notice in their bulletin each week saying that backpacks and similar bags are not allowed on the property. It also cautions that they will search any bag in question. When something appears to be suspicious, investigate. If you feel that a possible threat exists, call the authorities.

Early 2007
United States

Security personnel at a U.S. megachurch noticed a small group of men videotaping the exterior of their church. The local police arrived and, upon examination of the camera, discovered video scenes from schools, government buildings, utility plants and houses of worship. The police alerted the FBI, and the men left with federal authorities.

Another church reported that two men attempted to enter their worship center after the start of a Sunday morning service, carrying two clear plastic gallon jugs of what appeared to be water. When stopped by an usher, the men indicated that it was their drinking water. One of the containers was full, and the other was opened and about half full. The usher refused to let the men into the worship center with the water and offered to hold it for them. They finally agreed, giving the jugs to the usher, and walked down the hallway toward the next set of doors into the worship center. He didn't follow them. He called security, and when security arrived, the men had disappeared. The liquid in the containers turned out to be water. Was it a "dry run" to see if chemicals or explosives could be brought in without being challenged? The usher did a great job in not letting the liquid enter the worship center. However, someone should have followed the men.

Your ushers and greeters are part of your front-line security team. As a manner of extending God's love, they should greet everyone that comes in. Say hello, shake hands and, if someone is new, ask his or her name and where he or she is from. Remember, the "bad guys" don't want to be identified. If they are, they may not come back. If an usher feels that someone they've met is acting strangely, he or she should call security just to be safe. That feeling in the pit of the stomach happens for a reason. We never want to look back and say, "I wish I had called."

Don't allow vehicles to park next to your building. Meet with police and fire representatives to determine where you can paint fire lanes and no parking areas. Place vehicle barriers at entrances to your building or close to sidewalks. These could be bollards or large concrete planters. A great resource is the book *Crime Prevention Through Environmental Design* by Tim Crowe. The book shows how to incorporate security in building and property design.

WHAT TO DO

• Meet with Authorities

○ Meet with local law enforcement, EMS and fire department representatives. Also, check with your state's office of Homeland Security to learn how they may be able to help you.

• Ask for an On-Site Inspection

○ In the last few years, law enforcement, fire and EMS have accelerated training for a mass-casualty response. They all have someone that can make a visit and recommend ways to improve your safety and security program.

• "Harden" Your House of Worship

○ Make your facility more difficult to attack. Create a heightened sense of awareness among your staff and volunteers, especially greeters and ushers.

○ Ask the police how they would protect your buildings(s) from a vehicle attempting to drive/crash into it.

○ If someone drove by your complex, would he or she see evidence of a security presence? Is there a marked police vehicle parked there occasionally? Do you have a security company patrolling the area at night?

○ During regular office hours, be sure to lock all exterior doors. Large churches may keep a front entrance unlocked with a church staff member or volunteer staffing a reception desk. If needed, lock the front door and operate it with an intercom and electric buzzer with a video camera for your receptionist.

• Join Security Organizations

○ Become a member of the American Society for Industrial Security (ASIS) and Infragard. ASIS is the largest association of security professionals in the world. Most cities have chapters that meet monthly, and their annual conference is a must-attend. Infragard

is a group of local businesses that meet with local and federal law enforcement to share homeland security information. The FBI hosts Infragard, which currently has 82 chapters with more than 46,000 members.

- **Invite On-Site Training**
  - Your local police and fire agencies are always looking for places that will allow them to train. I have had the SWAT team, bomb squad and K-9 unit train in our buildings and on our property. Of course, most of the training occurs during late-night hours when no one is using the facility. What a great way for the teams to familiarize themselves with your facility in case an emergency arises.

- **Train**
  - I would recommend quarterly training sessions for your staff, greeters, ushers and parking lot attendants. Share up-to-date safety and security concerns and maintain a high sense of awareness.

KEEPING WATCH

Our houses of worship are open for members and visitors — visitors who may have emotional and psychological problems. Their often-harmless actions may mirror those of someone who seeks to do harm, like a suicide bomber. Always use caution and discernment when you are called to investigate, realizing that you could may be dealing with a person needing help ... or it could be a deadly threat.

- Train your ushers and greeters to recognize possible threats.

- Be alert to people videotaping or taking pictures of your church's exterior and interior. Visitors will tend to do this, so exercise discernment. Watch also for a person or group of people gathered in the same place each week observing others. Attacks are usually planned months in advance.

- Often, attackers appeared "suspicious," according to eyewitnesses and survivors.

- Look for the person who does not fit in. They may not be singing during worship or may be looking around and appearing nervous.

- Attackers may be dressed inappropriately for the situation or weather, such as wearing bulky winter clothes during summer.

- Carefully observe a person who makes an awkward attempt to blend in with a crowd or repeatedly and nervously handles parts of his or her clothing. Someone that might be planning to do harm may also avoid eye contact or quickly move away after establishing eye contact.

- Search all backpacks and bags that people carry into the sanctuary or worship center. If someone is seen acting suspiciously while entering any part of your complex with a backpack or purse, stop and search it. As stated earlier, some houses of worship do not allow any backpacks on the property.

Improvised Explosive Devices (IEDs)

Of the myriad ways that someone could employ an IED to attack a house of worship, I've come up with four that seem most logical. The four possible ways to inflict maximum damage would be a suicide bomber, a remotely detonated hidden device, a drone and a bomb-laden vehicle. There is no sure method of preventing an attack. However, if a target is too tough and hardened, most bombers will choose another target.

An incident that occurred in an Illinois church highlights our need to be vigilant:

Shortly before the 11 a.m. worship service on Sunday, the church's head usher observed a man carrying a briefcase and behaving suspiciously. He immediately communicated his concerns to other members of his team, the children's security team leader and the executive pastor. Security greeted the man as he entered the worship center and asked what was in the briefcase. The man said that there was a bomb in it. Church officials called 911 immediately, and an off-duty Sheriff's Deputy escorted the man out of the church.

Authorities isolated the briefcase outside and away from the church. A decision was made not to evacuate the building based on the fact that the threat had been moved outside, so the safest place for everyone was within the concrete walls of the church. While officers and church staff contained the situation within the building, the bomb squad decided to shoot the briefcase with a high-pressure water cannon. In case of an explosion, the pastor told the congregation that there might be a loud noise. He assured them that they were safe and not to leave the worship center.

As a secondary precaution, leaders in the children's department were told to move children to a safer location within the building and to warn the children of a possible loud noise. When police opened the briefcase, they found a Bible, a calculator and some miscellaneous items inside. They discovered no explosive device.

Hidden Devices

Walk the building before it is opened for services or events, searching for packages, bags, boxes or other items that appear unusual or out of place. Pay particular attention to the worship center and children's area. Have the same people performing the search each week, as they are more apt to notice something unusual or out of place.

Look for any items or packages left behind when cleaning the worship center between and after services. Report any findings to security.

Vehicle-Borne IEDs

IEDs come in many forms, from a simple pipe bomb to a large truck parked next to a building, as evidenced by the Oklahoma City bombing. Ensure a standoff distance for vehicles of at least 100 feet. Be aware of any unattended vehicles inhabiting "No Parking" areas.

Security Lighting

Install adequate security lighting. Always use "white" light so that video footage accurately conveys the colors of an attackers hair, clothes or vehicles. New LED lights are excellent in giving off light to protect and identify. Sodium lamps give off amber or orange light, which make most objects appear gray in color.

Maintain landscaping in a manner that will provide unobstructed lines of sight around your building(s).

SUMMARY OF TERRORISM

- Meet with authorities and invite them for a site visit.
- "Harden" your church against attack.
- Join local and national security organizations and associations.
- Train your staff and volunteers.
- Continually evaluate and improve your plans.

BIOGRAPHY

Ron Aguiar is an expert on safety and security for houses of worship. He has more than 30 years of experience in law enforcement and private security. Ron founded Oasis Safety in 2017 following his retirement after 19 years as director of safety and security at one of America's largest churches, Southeast Christian Church in Louisville, Kentucky. He also served for four years as safety and security director of Papa John's International. In addition, he has worked private security details from 2006 to 2019. Ron is a sought-after speaker and a consultant to houses of worship, para-church organizations and law enforcement agencies. He lives with his wife, Nancy, in Louisville, Kentucky. They have two grown children and one grandson.

Contact Information:
  Oasis Safety
  OasisSafety.com
  ron@oasissafety.com

NOTES